[RE]STITCH
TAMPA

**Designing the Post-War
Coastal American City
Through Ecologies**

Shannon Bassett

Acknowledgements

There are many people to thank for the (Re)Stitch Tampa project and this ensuing publication.

Foremost, I am grateful to the National Endowment for the Arts–Art Works initiative that made the (Re)Stitch Tampa project possible. It was a pleasure working with the wonderful staff there. I would also like to thank Maurice Cox, former Design Director for the National Endowment for the Arts, whom I first met when he was presenting at a workshop at the Structures for Inclusion Conference at the Harvard Graduate School of Design in 2008. Indeed, it was Maurice who first put the seed of an idea into my mind to propose a transformative design ideas competition for my adopted city of Tampa. I, of course, had no idea at the time how much of a monumental effort this would be, nor the life of its own that (Re)Stitch Tampa would take on. I would also like to thank the University of South Florida and the University at Buffalo SUNY for their institutional support.

A big shout-out must go to my USF student assistants. Without their help, this ambitious undertaking would not have been possible. Dan Roark was a graduate assistant extraordinaire for his tireless and boundless enthusiasm for the project. With his characteristic humor and energy, Dan was involved in every phase of (Re) Stitch Tampa up to the end, including its finest details. This included selecting an ambient soundtrack to accompany the competition's launch at the Tampa Museum of Art, chauffeuring and hosting our esteemed jurors, and putting the finishing touches on the competition exhibit at USF CAMLS in downtown Tampa. This exhibit served as a public forum and a tool for helping the public to envision a Tampa reconnected to its River, as portrayed in the competition entries, through design excellence. Dan also developed many of the iconic graphics which were an important part of the competition's communication. Jessica Antonen was an on-point project (task)manager who cleverly devised an innovative social media campaign to disseminate the competition call to the many far flung corners of the globe. This call was seminal to the diverse and unexpected global response to the competition and to the many countries represented in the cross-section of design proposals. Rayane Plyler was also a critical contributor to many of the striking iconic graphics for the competition. Matt Gaboury built a robust website for the (Re)Stitch Tampa competition, which served as the critical interface for both disseminating, as well as managing the competition. This website now continues to function as a digital archive of the project, serving not only as a showcase of the winning schemes, but now as a graphic historical narrative describing key urban issues in Tampa Bay at that specifically charged and challenging period in its urban history. Josh Figueroa also helped to host our jurors and to set up the final exhibit at USF CAMLS, as did Stephen Benson. Thank you to all these outstanding students.

I extend a warm thanks to our international jurors who I was delighted to learn had agreed to participate in the (Re) Stitch Tampa project. They include Margaret Crawford,

Chad Oppenheim, Juhani Palasmaa, Chris Reed-STOSS and Charles Waldheim. Your insights and comments regarding the proposals, as well as the lively discussions leading to those selected as winners and honorable mentions were stimulating and enriching to be a part of. On awards day, audience members included the general public, the constituents, stakeholders and elected officials, as well as students and educators. The lectures delivered by the international jurors on that day, included discussion of the critical frameworks of the specific competition, but also set its issues as part of a larger contemporary discourse on the potential for ecological urbanism when addressing the challenges of designing post war city urbanism. This discussion was welcomed by the Tampanian public who are faced with these very real challenges of the post-war city, and are personally impacted by a number of the urban episodes and ruptures as were framed in the competition. I am likewise grateful to our local Tampa and Florida jurors, including Councilwoman Lisa J. Montelione, Laurier Potier-Brown, Ray Chiaramonte of the Tampa Planning Authority and Emily O'Mahoney, former Florida ASLA President, whose ongoing tireless dedication to the city of Tampa is evident.

Thanks also to Lee Hoffman, Riverwalk Manager for the City of Tampa, for his continued involvement in the (re) stitching of Tampa to its river, and for continuing to link the implementation of the ongoing Tampa Riverwalk construction, as an important public space in the city, to the ideas and discourse generated by the ideas competition. I will always fondly remember the boat tour that Lee narrated for our visiting jurors on the day of the Competition Awards Ceremony. As we waited in the boat, President Obama's car entourage sped by on the bridge above. He was, coincidentally, visiting the city of Tampa the same day as our awards ceremony. This was especially coincidental as his initiative for the high-speed rail project in Florida was the impetus of the competition's framework. (Sadly, however, the high-speed rail was not implemented.)

I am also appreciative for the groundswell of local support: from the American Institute of Architects (AIA) Tampa Bay, Dawn Madges and Jessica Smith, from the USF College of the Arts, Karen Franck, Trent Green Ron Chandler and Martha Sherman from the USF School of Architecture and Community Design, Captain Larry from Captain Larry's Water Taxi, Lorraine Suarez and Tom Levin, Landscape Architect from Ekistics, the Florida Chapter of the American Society of Landscape Architects, from LDC International Inc., Antonio Amadeo and Ryan Murphy, MLI Integrated Graphic Solutions, The Office of Sustainability at the University of South Florida, the Suncoast Chapter of the American Planning Association (APA), the Sustany Foundation, the Tampa Downtown Partnership, the Tampa Museum of Art and 83 Degrees Media. We were privileged to display the final panels of the competition at the USF CAMLS Medical Center where its wonderful venue served as a public forum to disseminate the design ideas.

I would also like to acknowledge the elegant and inspiring Lena Young and the Tampa Green Artery, whose grass-roots community activism, in the true sense of the word, is demonstrated through their tireless and relentless devotion to connect the Hillsborough River to Tampa's community green spaces. Their zealous work with communities and neighborhood parks continues to be an inspiration.

I extend a huge thanks to ACTAR publishers for undertaking the publication of this project. Thanks to Editor Ricardo Devesa, Ramon Prat, Graphic Designer Lucía López Casanegra and Brian Brash and who, through their beautiful work, have enabled me to realize this (Re) Stitch Tampa publication.

I also give thanks to my parents, Susan and Des Bassett, for their unconditional love, support and encouragement through my numerous life-defining moments and challenges.

Perhaps the largest thanks must go to all of those who submitted their wonderful design ideas competitions to (Re) Stitch Tampa. Design entries came from almost forty different teams representing over 15 different countries around the world. It is you who made this possible. Your cross-cultural lenses from your different perspectives brought forth many insights of possible design strategies for the American post-war coastal city.

And finally, I must recognize the dolphins and manatee of the Tampa Bay who sometimes swim up the Hillsborough River from the Tampa Bay and its estuary, to emerge at unexpected and incredible moments in the River, in the middle of the city, almost surreally juxtaposed against the post-war city skyline. They serve as reminders that nature, habitat and ecologies continue to be part of our cities, sometimes in spite of our human indifference to their beauty, and that we must advocate, if not fight, for designing our cities in harmony with them and the multitude of other eco-systems and the services they provide to us all.

ART WORKS.
arts.gov

Index

[re]stitch TAMPA
an international ideas competition

launching **09.01.11!**
www.restitchtampa.org

ART WORKS.
arts.gov

USF
UNIVERSITY OF
SOUTH FLORIDA
COLLEGE OF THE ARTS

University of South Florida
School of Architecture and Community Design
c/o [re]stitch TAMPA
4202 East Fowler Avenue, HMS 301
Tampa, Florida 33620

[re]stitchTAMPA to its Riverfront is an international Ideas competition for the city of Tampa which calls for proposals envisioning a new design for the city's civic realm through connective urban landscapes and landscape infrastructure which [re]stitches the city back to its river and brings the river back into the city. The findings of the competition will be a catalyst for the shaping of future development of the waterfront and the designing of public urban spaces of the city. The competition will be judged by a confirmed renowned international jury, as well as local stakeholders, and includes competition prize money.

Dates to Remember:
09/01/2011   Competition launch and on-line registration begins
12/2011   First stage competition due and First Stage winners announced
04/2012   Second stage competition due
04/2012   Awards ceremony

Sponsored, in part, by a grant from the National Endowment for the Arts-Access to Artistic Excellence and the University of South Florida School of Architecture and Community Design. Visit our website for updates.

launching **09.01.11!**
www.restitchtampa.org

Competition Brief

www.restitchtampa.org

Launched: Sept. 1, 2011
Tampa Museum of Art, downtown Tampa

Awards Ceremony:
April 13, 2012 - Downtown Tampa

DESIGN CHARGE FROM THE ORIGINAL COMPETITION BRIEF

(Re)Stitch Tampa is an international ideas competition for the city of Tampa. The competition calls for innovative design ideas, which employ connective urban landscapes and ecological infrastructure as an underlying urban design framework. This urban framework can act as a catalyst for the economic redevelopment for Tampa, while physically reconnecting a currently disparate and fragmented city and community.

(Re)Stitch Tampa calls for design ideas, which reconsider infrastructure and how it might be a transformative urban design agent as the underlying connective tissue and network which (re) stitches the city to its river, and brings the river into the city.

DESIGN CHANGE

The Obama Administration's announcement, in the beginning of 2010, of 1.25 billion dollars of federal monies earmarked for a High-speed rail connection between Orlando and Tampa, to be the first high speed train in the United States, was a catalyst for the re-thinking of a large-scale infrastructural re-designing for the city. While in the end the High-speed rail project was not implemented, as the federal monies for it were returned by the state governor to the feder-

1

al government, this infrastructural initiative still prompted the momentum for a critical rethinking of an infrastructural re-design for the city. How might this framework begin to choreograph the flows and the movements through the city, to and from the river, through urbanism and place-making? An urban design master plan, which was initially to be focused around the expected High-speed rail station area, can now provide the impetus of re-thinking infrastructure, which can connect the city back to its River.

HISTORY

The urban condition of Tampa is a unique and specific one, different from many urban precedents currently written about in textbooks, which focus primarily on northern American cities whose urban morphology was influenced by traditional European cities with centers. Tampa is a car-oriented city, suffering from the impacts of suburban sprawl, a largely poly-nucleated city with a shrinking downtown. The downtown core was heavily impacted by 1950ies urban renewal strategies carried out in the 60'ies and 70ies, as well as heavy-handed highway infrastructural development which fractured a culturally vibrant downtown core with overhead expressways. This enabled a mass suburban exodus to the sprawling suburbs, eating up valuable agricultural lands and wetlands. The downtown Central Business District (CBD), which empties out after 5pm and on weekends, has a distinctly rural-urban condition, which includes over 50% surface parking lots. Preceding this, the 2008 financial crash and mortgage crisis had hit both Tampa and Florida excessively hard due to their direct economic link to real-estate speculation and "flipping".

The vacancies of both the existing brownfields and gray fields are now accompanied by the red fields of foreclosure lots, including land banking or plats assembled by developers, which have not been developed and currently lie in bankruptcy.

The Hillsborough River or the "Blue Artery", is a natural amenity running through the city, currently occupying no great presence within the city's DNA. It has a large watershed, which empties into the Tampa Bay on the west side of the downtown core, forming a "U" around the southern tip of the city alongside the Channelside Shipping Channel. Furthermore, the city is largely fractured from its waterfront due to a legacy of heavy-handed, car-privileging infrastructure, as well as a lack of pedestrian connectivity and civic spaces linking the city grid to the River.

ECOLOGY

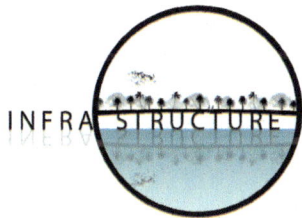
INFRASTRUCTURE

CONNECTIVITY

3

COMPETITION FRAMEWORK AND CALL FOR DESIGN STRATEGIES

The objectives of this design ideas competition are to critically re-claim, as well as to re-think the city's current infrastructure.

The framework outlines an integrated approach with respect to:

Ecology + Infrastructure + Connectivity

DESIGN AND SITE

The boundaries of the Riverwalk site for intervention are from the North Street Bridge at the north end of the Riverwalk, to the Channelside District, which is located at the south end of the Riverwalk.

Please refer to diagram, "Primary Area of Concern", (located in the Drawing and Resource Section) for boundaries of intervention. The intervention at the River should extend the length of the footprint of the current Riverwalk, and to the public right of way, which extends from the North Street Bridge at the north down to Channelside, as outlined on the diagram. The immediate adjacencies should be considered as opportunities for possible (re)stitching strategies. While the River should be conceptualized as the new center for the city, the current area for emphasis for proposed design strategies should be on the east side of the river, with connections to "Neighborhood Districts" and "Points of Interest" (Please refer to these diagrams of the same name in the Drawings and Resources Section Under "Diagrams").

ECOLOGY - THE RIVER + ITS ECOLOGIES

The Hillsborough River as Palimpsest

The Hillsborough River is the main organizing spine for the design proposal, as well as the catalyst for the proposed design strategies.

The competition encourages strategies which propose connective urban landscapes, which dual both as ecological infrastructure, as well as place-makers. For example, a storm-water management system using landscape infrastructure can also function as an open-space system, which creates a connective pedestrian network with recreational activities. Therein also lies the possibility of addressing the various ecological issues inherent to the Hillsborough River along its urban watershed.

At the end of the 19th century, people came from all over the region to eat the oysters and clams out of the Hillsborough River and the Tampa Bay. Today, the city's storm drains and culverts empty directly into the river. The river has a large watershed, and is significantly impacted by the amount of rain and precipitation that Tampa experiences annually. Storm water runoff from the street flows from the land into the river. Storm water mitigation began in the 1960ies and 1970ies. The river itself is also susceptible to sea level rise, and has been documented to have risen 10 inches since the 1960ies. It is also susceptible to the storm surge from the Tampa Bay with its tributaries.

Shore softening strategies are currently occurring, albeit in fragmented locations, along the entire Hillsborough River within the city. Some of these strategies have been initiated to reintroduce biodiversity to the river, with shoreline and habitat restoration, in addition to fish and bird habitat. This has involved the removal of the past existing dilapidated seawall, a leftover relic from the River's industrial past. Manatees have been spotted in some of the River's locations, drawn to spring-fed parts of the river such as Sulphur Springs. Strategies to re-introduce natural habitats such as oyster beds and mussels have also acted as low-impact filtration and cleaning mechanisms for cleaning the river water. Plants such as marsh grasses, which can withstand different salinity levels, also provide the eco-system services of reducing some of the nutrients that are the byproducts of the runoff going into the river, including algae. Natural reefs and rip-rip such as limestone, oyster shells and reef balls, have been re-introduced in place of the hard seawall infrastructure, acting as substrates and reefs which allow natural habitats to occur.

The sharp economic downturn in real estate resulting from the 2008 financial crash and mortgage crisis, from which Tampa has been particularly impacted, has left several assembled parcels by developers along the river vacant and unoccupied. Redfields of foreclosed properties have now been aggregated with brownfields and grayfields. Paradoxically, this has actually strengthened and returned a robust ecology and biodiversity along the River's edge, subsequently dissolving the city grid at the river into a recovered edge landscape.

Design schemes for the river should integrate sustainable sites initiatives such as low impact design (LID) through urban landscape and ecological infrastructure. These might inform new development guidelines for the possible future development of the river's urban site and watershed. Such strategies should foster new relationships to landscape ecology and biodiversity within an urban condition, in addition to serving as a didactic tool for the schools located in the area along the river. Design proposals should simultaneously extend this line of thinking beyond the river's spine and into the city's infrastructural system, including its current grid system. For example, a functioning water management system such as bio-swales, which can clean water before running off the street into the river, might also attract native habitat within the city such as butterflies and native clams, etc.

Proposed design strategies should also address the ecological issues that the river faces. These strategies should mitigate against storm water run-off and pollutants going directly into the Hillsborough River. This might also might include the restoration of natural habitats and ecologies and biodiversity along the river, which currently exist in certain locations. This provides an opportunity, where the grid meets the returning natural systems, for a new alternative form of development, existing not only as aesthetic landscapes, but also as bioregional habitats and ecologies within urban habitat.

Through the creation of a connective, ecological infrastructural tissue between the city and the river, layered programming should be proposed in design schemes. These should also possess a certain level of flexibility and indeterminacy within its design. Some of these programs should also include building an environmental and art and wellness awareness, in addition to strengthening the pedestrian connections, which are currently under-developed in the city. Other possible programming can include place-making, as well as recreational and cultural activities. "The Tampa Green Artery", one of the stakeholder groups of the River, is currently looking at ways in order to implement a Green Artery through the city which connects its green spaces. While locating this Green Artery along the Hillsborough River would be the logical area, there exists currently only a public right of way along the stretch of River that the Riverwalk currently occupies.

INFRASTRUCTURE

The River, initially the lifeline for the city and the reason for its initial siting, reveals its post-industrial landscape and palimpsest through visible remnants of its former life as an industrial and working river infrastructure for the city. These remnants include its decaying seawall, some remaining Atlantic Coast rail infrastructure, as well as key industrial buildings such as the Tampa Trolley Barn/Armature Works located south of the North Street Bridge at the north end of the Riverwalk. Heavy-handed and car privileging infrastructure dramatically transformed the urban landscape during the period of urban renewal in Tampa, occurring in the 1960ies.

The design proposal should demonstrate a re-thinking of current infrastructures within the intervention area, as well as proposing a matrix, which reconceptualizes them. The river has been reconceptualised by the city from its post-industrial landscape of a working river, to an economic development engine for the city. Therein also lies the opportunity of introducing a landscape and ecological infrastructure which can provide a public right of way, as well as remediation and water cleaning for water management infrastructure and a buffer for sea level rise, in addition to producing local economies with the restoration of natural and plant and animal habitats including fish, clams and oysters and algae production.

The former rail line, which ran along the river in the city, has now become a cultural and institutional spine, with the Rivergate Tower and the decaying elevated Kiley Gardens beside it. The Tampa Art Museum, the Children's Museum, the main branch of the city library, as well as the Straz Performance Art center are located to the North. This cultural swatch lies between the Hillsborough River and Ashley Drive to the East. It is bordered by Kennedy Street, Tampa's initial main street, to the south and to the North is bordered by the 275 highway. This has caused the cultural swatch to remain fractured from the city due to an off-ramp from the 275 which brings cars into the city along Ashley Drive, at highway speeds which produce daunting crossings for pedestrians attempting to access the Riverwalk from the city grid and its Central Business District (CBD). Some successful urban stitches have begun at the new Curtis Hixon Park in between the Tampa Art Museum,

as well as the Children's Museum and Rivergate tower which have layered urban functions and programming on them. The CSX train line runs alongside the Tampa Art Museum and the river. The location of the site initially acquired and assembled for the High-speed rail station was designated to be a multi-modal station, which could include bus rapid transit and possibly, at a future date, light rail. Streets are car privileging, and many of the main streets running through the downtown core should undergo the "skinnying" of their widths or "street diets," as they are often four lane one-way streets where cars speed through the city. These are hazards and are non-conducive to viable public and pedestrian realm. Several bridge infrastructures cross over the river. Here, then, lie some issues for crossing underneath them with the Riverwalk, which might necessitate floating infrastructures.

6-8

Suggested Infrastructures for Design proposal

- Water taxi infrastructure along the river (past studies have proposed both local neighborhood service, in addition to a regional taxi service servicing across the Tampa Bay to St. Petersburg

- Bicycle and Pedestrian Infrastructure

- Boating and Floating Infrastructure

- Landscape and Ecological Infrastructures

- Water Management Infrastructure, which addresses city storm water collection, as well as mitigation through possible landscape infrastructure strategies

- Open-Space Infrastructure, which allows for a multiplicity of different and layered programs and indeterminacy with the potential to connect to a currently fragmented existing open space system.

- Shade Infrastructure

- Re-Engagement of Bridge Infrastructure with existing Bridge Crossings over the Hillsborough River

CONNECTIVITY

The design charge is that of an overall infrastructural strategy for the re-connection of a former post-industrial waterfront landscape to the city, which is currently being developed as an arts/cultural spine. Connections will be through a connective urban landscape and ecological infrastructure, providing connections from the city to the river, and by bringing the river into the city. Existing infrastructure should be re-considered and re-programmed, allowing for multiple purposes and indeterminate surfaces and programs, which can be juxtaposed alongside each other. Connections can begin to be made which stretch the river infrastructure into the city, in order to connect major points, nodes and districts.

A legacy of incremental and short-sighted planning and policy decisions over time with respect to infrastructure over its past history, have had the compounded impact of the fracturing of the city's connectivity between the river, furthering the disconnect of the city to the river and the river to the city. The design proposal should advance alternative infrastructures en lieu of the current car-oriented infrastructures with the intent of advocating for the public realm, health and wellness, in addition to providing eco-system services.

Interstitial space in between the new Tampa art museum and the Rivergate tower and defunct Kiley Gardens.

Design proposals should consider how an infrastructure proposal can begin to remediate and act as the salve to heal these incisions within the urban and ecological landscapes, as well as identifying major pathways of connections.

Connectivity should be made to vibrant neighborhoods with adjacencies including:

Tampa Heights with the iconic Tampa Armature building Trolley Barn and Waterworks building with the Ulele natural spring, the city's first source of drinking water, being restored and reconnected to the river. Tampa Heights was the first trolley suburb of Tampa. River lots were assembled for development by developers and now remain vacant and under foreclosure.

The Encore Housing project is a mixed-use housing project with both market rate, as well as affordable housing on the eastern edge of downtown of the land assembled for the high-speed rail station, and now anticipated multi-modal station with possible bus rapid transit and light rail. The site was formally a vibrant African American and African Cuban neighborhood called "the Scrub" know for its jazz music, which was razed during the period of Urban Renewal and slum clearance and replaced by public housing projects.

The Channelside District is a new neighborhood of warehouses and loft spaces adjacent to the dredged Ybor Shipping Channel.

Outlying Connections

Ybor City lies at the eastern edge of the downtown core and was historically predominantly Cuban and Italian and the location for the cigar rolling industry. It still has iconic cigar factories and the historic Cuban and Italian Clubs.

Hyde Park is a historical trolley suburb of Tampa adjacent to the Bayshore pathway which is an active pedestrian and bikeway along a hard sea wall. The proposed connector of these urban infrastructural systems would be across the Platt Street bridge to the southwest of the main segment of the north-south running Riverwalk.

SUGGESTED PROGRAMS

Submittal Requirements

This competition is an urban design ideas competition. The main focus is the river as the spine for the city.

Concepts should illustrate proposals such as concepts operating at the level of catalytic urban strategies and proposals through the three lenses described in the framework above, "Ecology", "Infrastructure" and "Connectivity", as well as describing possible design guidelines with a priority on the re-thinking and re-porgramming of infrastructures. Entries can make suggestions for massing scenarios of possible building fabric, but these should remain at a schematic massing level and be descriptive of design strategies and guidelines for it if it is the intent that design strategies should propose an overall infrastructural strategies, as well as crafting urban, landscape and ecological infrastructure guidelines for the city, which could inform all subsequent development and infill projects, as well as implementation.

9

10

11

1. Mappings of Parking Lots - Over 50% Parking Lots with Vacancies in Tampa's Downtown Core.
2. Tampa's Post-Industrial Waterfront as Viewed from the Hillsborough River.
3. Competition Framework Framed through Ecology-Infrastructure -Connectivity.
4. Crosstown Expressway Highway Infrastructures Spans over the Hillsborough River along Tampa's Post-Industrial Waterfront.
5. Tampa Armature Works-Trolley Barn and Post-Industrial Landscape. Interfaces with Softened Edge of Reclaimed Ecological Landscape.
6-8. City Views.
9. Section through Tampa's Urban Ecologies.
10. Tampa's Post-Industrial Waterfront, Tampa, Florida, With its Natural Ecologies-Returning the Industrial Waterfront back to its Natural Shoreline with the Advent of Foreclosure Lots and Bankruptcies.
11. Program Icons with Ecological and Sustainable Functions.

1. Tampa Skyline from Cass St. Bridge from a softened, ecological
and post-industrial landscape.
2. Channelside and Port Terminal.
3. Downtown Tampa skyline from Armature Works/Tampa Trolley Barn
from post-industrial pier relic.

4

5

4. Tampa Armature Works-Trolley Barn Post-Industrial Landscape Interfaces with Naturalized Landscape.
5. Arts and Cultural Spine-Tampa Art Museum and Curtis Hixon Park along the Hillsborough River.
6. West View from Cotanchobee Fort Brooke Park.

7. Kiley Gardens and Rivergate Tower.
8. University of Tampa from Kennedy St. Bridge.
9. South View from Expressway towards Convention Centre.

HISTORIC SITE

Images all courtesy of the Burgert Brother Collection, Special & Digital Collections, Tampa Library, University of South Florida and Courtesy of the Tampa-Hillsborough County Public Library System.

1. Automobile traffic on Bayshore Boulevard looking northeast - 1922.
2. Franklin Street, intersection with Polk Street, view north with automobile and pedestrian traffic and the F.W. Woolworth Company and Kress department stores - 1956.
3. Downtown area and the eastern bank of the Hillsborough River, aerial view - 1957.

4

5

6

4,5. Sailing ships docked at Lee Terminal at the Port of Tampa - 1919.
6. Trolley car on Lafayette Street passing near Hyde Park Avenue - 1918.
7. Downtown area and the eastern bank of the Hillsborough River, aerial view - 1957.
8. Downtown Tampa view northeast from Florida Avenue to Hillsborough County Courthouse on Madison Street - 1954.
9. Downtown Tampa skyline and railroad yard on east bank of Hillsborough River viewed from vicinity of Cass Street railroad bridge - 1925.

10. Tampa Skyline from Plant Hotel viewing former rail infrastructure alone the Hillsborough River-Atlantic Coast line.
11. Boating on the Sulfur Spring.
12. Automobiles turning onto the Platt Street Bridge from Bayshore Boulevard - 1939.

Mappings

**Ecological Mappings od Cypress ans Mandgrove Forest
within the Hillsborough River Watershed**

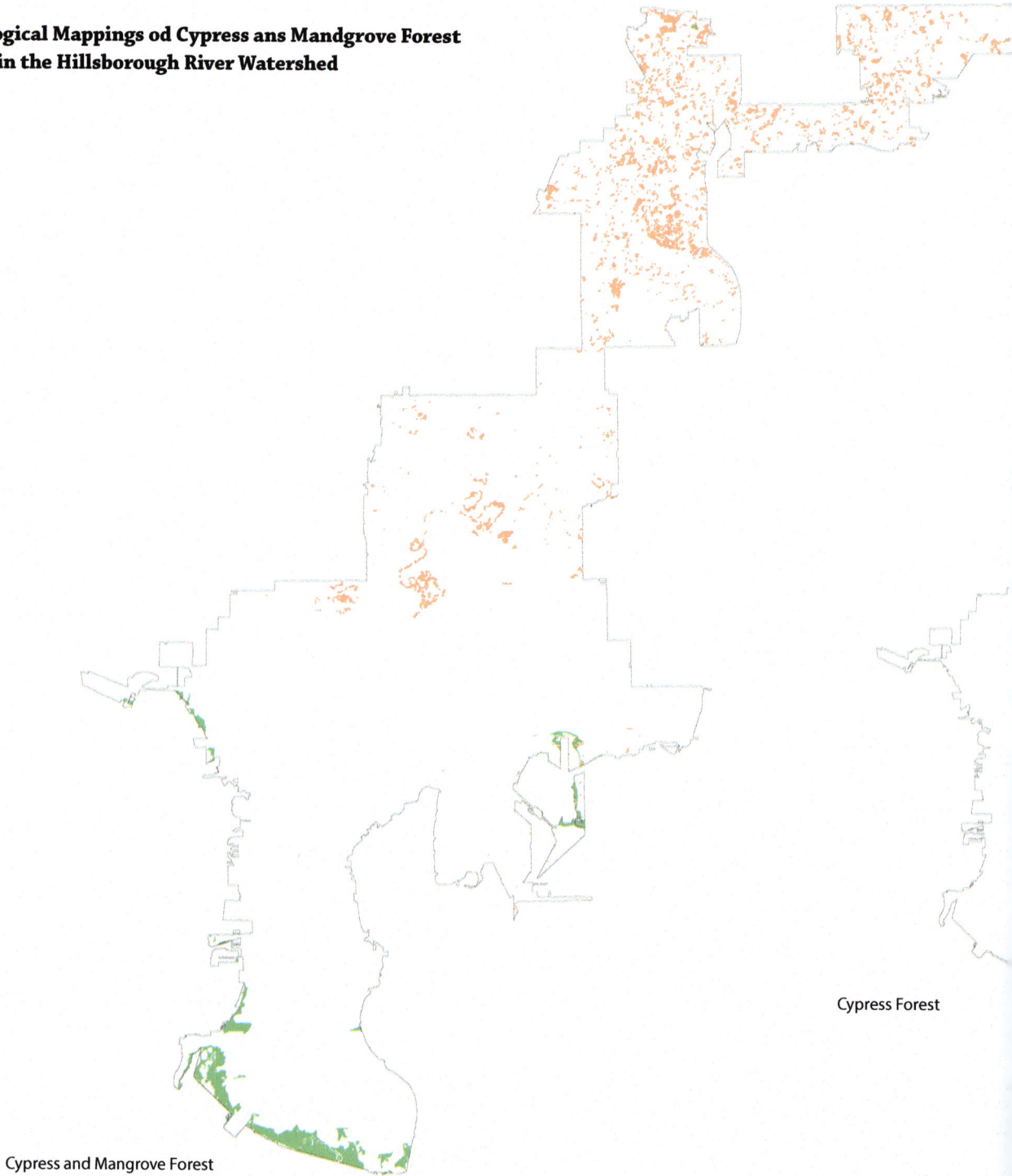

Cypress Forest

Cypress and Mangrove Forest

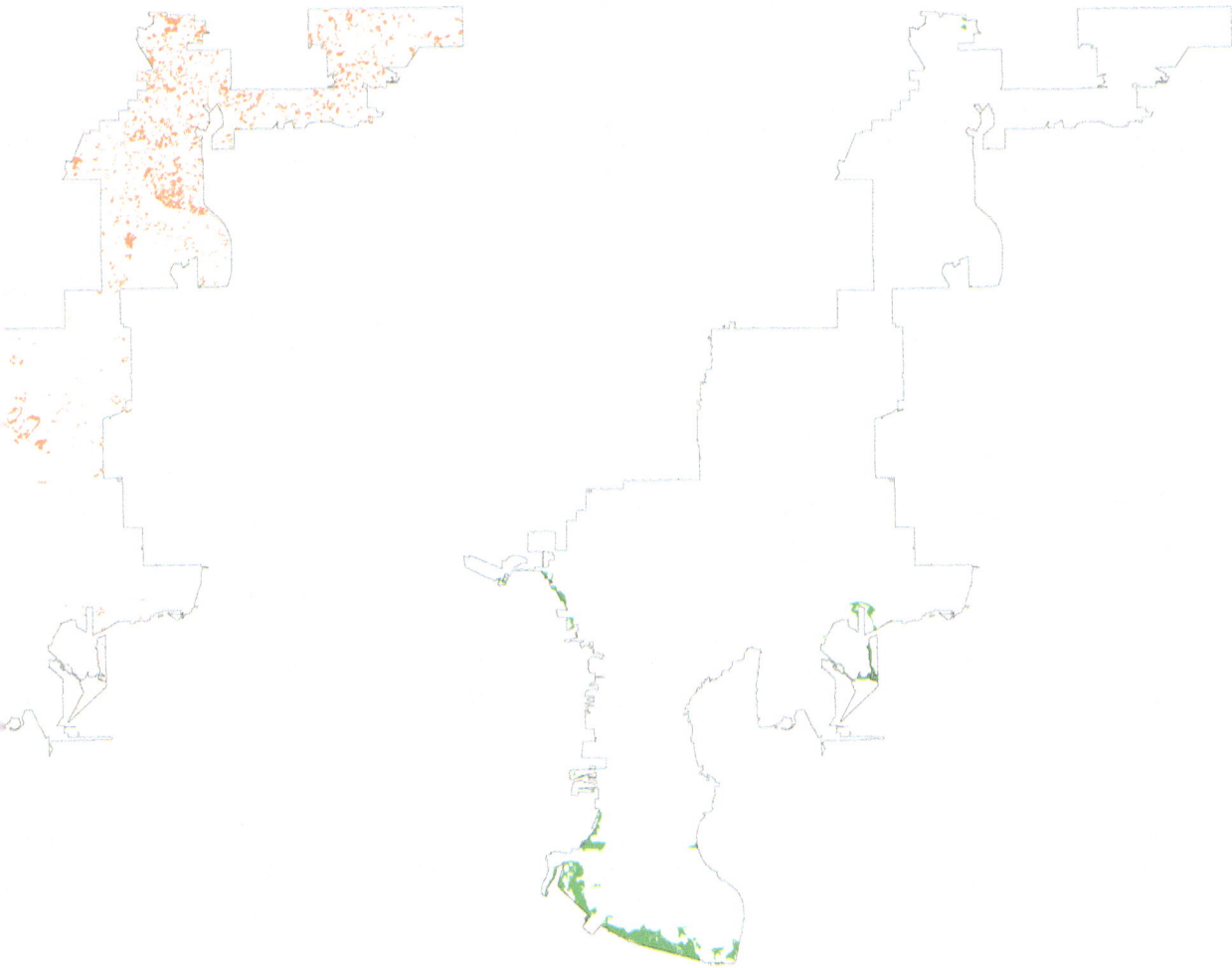

Mangrove Forest

Hillsborough River

Hillsborough River Street Grid Diagram

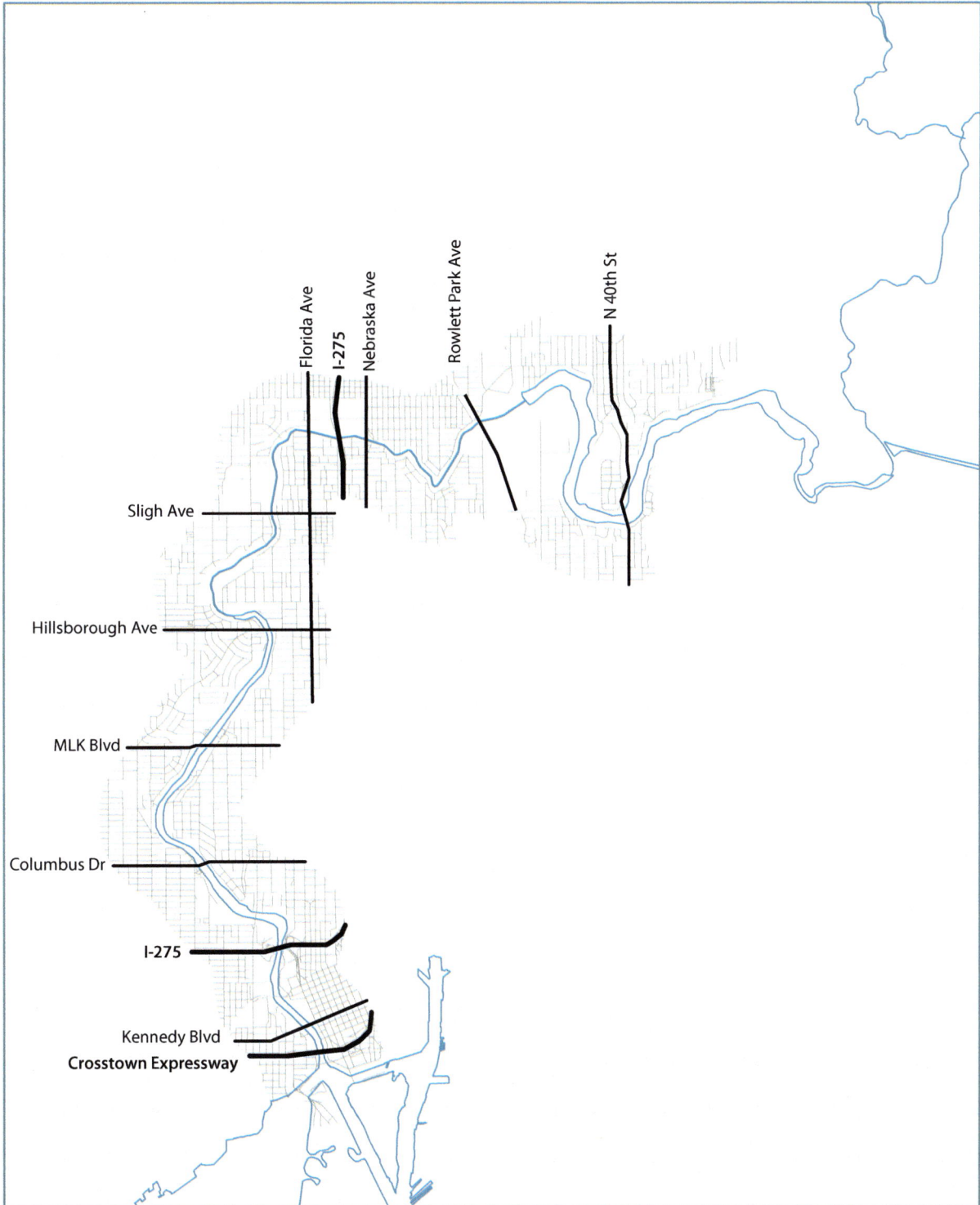

Florida Ave

I-275

Nebraska Ave

Rowlett Park Ave

N 40th St

Sligh Ave

Hillsborough Ave

MLK Blvd

Columbus Dr

I-275

Kennedy Blvd

Crosstown Expressway

Tampa as the Ecological City

Living with and Inhabiting the Estuary and the Swamp

Shannon Bassett

Architect and Uban Designer

INTRODUCTION

The (Re) Stitch Tampa project was initially conceptualized during 2010 around the advent of the announcement of what was to be the first high-speed rail line in the US. The Obama Administration had just announced as part of its "New" New Deal program, that the region was to receive 1.2 billion dollars in federal monies earmarked for the construction of a high-speed rail line along the Tampa-Orlando corridor. The program was reminiscent of Franklin D. Roosevelt's WPA program, during the great Depression, where the federal government funded large-scale public infrastructural projects with the intent of jump-starting the economy. In Florida, such projects included the Rural Electrification Program of rural farms, running wire to over 54,000 farms, and the development of much of the Florida State Park System. [1]

Tampa, a post-war coastal American city, was reeling from the worst recession since the great Depression. Arguably, it was also located in one of the regions the greatest impacted in the country by the 2008 economic bust and mortgage crisis. The region had developed around car privileging infrastructures and an economy predicated principally on real estate and its speculative practices. The real-estate bubble had burst hard here, where real-estate speculation and flipping were part of the main sources of the economy. It was not uncommon, beginning in 2007 and continuing onwards, to see hand-crafted signs dotting the on and off ramps of Tampa's highway infrastructures and byways of the city advertising short-sale, foreclosed houses, or offering flat-out cash for houses. *"We buy up houses-$50,000.00 each and 3 for..."* [2]

By 2011, however, this "New" New Deal in the form of high-speed rail infrastructure had been squashed, and the 1.2 billion dollars of federal monies returned to the federal government. The stymying of the project had been largely due to the prevailing anti-smart and, arguably, anti-urban politics which did not support the funding of public transportation. This was even despite the efforts of mayors in the 6 cities who would be positively impacted by the high-speed rail system, who self-organized at a local-regional level to accept the federal monies, although in the end they were not able to do so. The aggregated land for the high-speed rail station in Tampa was also left vacant, left to return back to nature. Therein existed other such aggregated plots of land or "land-banking" which had occurred at the height of the real-estate boom, such as on the north end of the Riverwalk, the northern anchor of the competition project site, where the developer had acquired and aggregated land and had then, subsequently, gone bankrupt. The Trolley Barn- Armature Works lay in decay, as a relic of the post-industrial landscape, and the former affluent trolley-car suburb and trolley system which was one of the most successful in the US before it was ripped-up and replaced by the roads of the predominant automobile culture. This aggregated lot lay in urban decay; the ecology and the bio-diversity returning back to it and recovering the site's natural landscape. This urban aggregate added to the 50% of surface parking, as well as to the additional vacancies in the downtown core.

The focus of the competition brief shifted, at this moment, to a critical re-thinking of the ebbs and flows of circulation and movement throughout the city, and how these might contribute to more sustainable development and ecological practices. The competition brief posed the question, how might the re-calibrating of infrastructure serve as an opportunity to re-choreograph the flows and the movements of people and habitat to and from its natural lifeline running through the city, and how might it bring the River into the city?

 Paradoxically, the recession and the mortgage crisis with its foreclosures, vacancies, and halted development, had actually provided an opportunity to take stock, as well as to critically reassess a legacy during the 20th century of largely unsustainable building and development practices and seemingly unlimited growth, much of which was eating up valuable wetlands and ecologically sensitive lands. Unsustainable land development practices had been catalyzed by the rationalization of the pumping system. Dredging, as well as the canalization of swamplands pushed by real-estate spec-

ulation and tourism, had largely trashed the natural environment and its ecologies. Further, the invention of air conditioning had perpetuated the development of housing typologies divorced from their natural systems and local ecologies, dissimilar to Florida's earlier vernacular housing typologies, such as the Florida Dogtrot. The Dogtrot's design was more integrated with passive design strategies, such as breezeways as well as the natural Florida landscape. The competition also prompted a re-thinking of the current oppositional relationship of the city to its water, as well as the potential to re-stitch, re-cover and re-claim the landscape of the Post-War Coastal American City through Ecologies.

TAMPA- THE BEGINNINGS OF THE POST-WAR COASTAL AMERICAN CITY

Unlike their counterparts to the North, the Sunbelt coastal cities of the south, including Tampa, did not experience the same overarching opposition to the top-down urban renewal planning practices of the 1950ies, largely inspired by the Modernist City. During the 1960ies, freeway revolts occurred in many American cities, opposing the byproducts of the 1958 Federal Highway Act, which included cutting highway infrastructure through swathes of the city in order to expedite commuters out to the suburbs. The post-war suburbs had been federally subsidized in the form of inexpensive mortgages to returning war vets from World War Two. Jane Jacobs, author of the seminal text, "The Death and Life of Great American Cities", successfully organized her community to oppose and subsequently defeat Robert Moses' attempt to bulldoze part of the West Village in New York City with a crosstown expressway infrastructure. Further, grass-roots community opposition to urban renewal projects and the bulldozing of Boston's historic West End and Scollay Square, as well as New York City's Penn Station, lay the groundwork for the bottom-up preservation movement of cities and their historic fabric beginning in the 1950ies. It also ushered in the establishment of the National Park Service in the US. Tampa's period of urban renewal happened later, in the 1960ies and 70ies. Unlike their northern counterparts, many of the community leaders in the districts designated for urban renewal, actually embraced it, as opposed to attempting to fight it, such as in Tampa's Ybor City. As Tampa historian Emanuel Leto writes, "these projects were also motivated, in part, by racial divisions within urban communities, and the desire for segregation in districts and enclaves of the city."[3] The erasure of one such community known as "the Scrub", was one of the three major urban renewal projects carried out by Tampa in the 1960ies as part of the Federal Urban Renewal program. Its name came from its natural landscape, referring to the territory outside of the protected Fort Brooke boundary which was settled by white settlers, and referred to the small brush-like vegetation of scrub and Florida brush. The area was settled by freed African-American slaves and the neighborhood had a vibrant music scene, including Ray Charles and Ella Fitzgerald. The inhabitants were re-located to public housing and the city became largely zoned as single use as part of the CBD (Central Business District), with highway infrastructure cutting through the urban fabric, carrying people out to the suburbs in the wetlands and the reclaimed swamplands, which lay beyond a middle landscape of trolley suburbs, largely vacated.

TAMPA AS THE ECOLOGICAL CITY

Prior to the period of urban renewal which radically transformed the urban space and fabric of Tampa, the settlement of the area had a much more intrinsic relationship to the landscape and its natural ecologies, living more symbiotically with the Tampa Bay natural estuary. Historical natural atlases and guides of Tampa from the turn of the 20th century boasted in their descriptions of Tampa's natural landscape, as well as its estuary. "People came from miles around to eat the fish and oysters out of the Tampa Bay". Such sites as Sulphur Springs, located further north up the Hillsborough River were, in fact, natural springs where people came from afar for their natural healing powers. Other sites of intrigue included an alligator farm adjacent to the natural spring. The site became contaminated and trashed in the middle part of the 20th century, however, although ecological remediation and recovery is currently being undertaken in the area by the City.

The competition brief is premised on a critique of the failings of the post-war American City, the prevailing traces and conditions of which can be seen in Tampa. The brief also calls for resilient design strategies, which address its coastal location, as well as the re-articulation of its land-water edge between the city and the water. It proposes possible design strategies, which might begin to de-construct, de-engineer, as well as to de-laminate the previous infrastructures that are part of the legacy of these predominantly short-sited planning strategies. The competition framed a re-thinking and re-programming, as well as the re-articulation and re-consideration of the possible occupation of infrastructures operating at a large-scale.

(Re)stitch Tampa serves as a research platform. The publication serves as a useful toolkit and handbook for disseminating design strategies which both design for resiliency, as well as addressing the conditions which are resultant from the failings of the policies around the post-war American city, and their unintended consequences. Designers are trained to be strategic, innovative and tactical in design, as well as having the ability to synthesize multi-scalar systems, and to conceptualize multiple scenarios for different conditions.

The brief also encouraged designers to work across a spectrum of design scales, while addressing issues of recovering a landscape. Arguably, the state of Florida and its coastal cities will be some of those the worst impacted in the US by sea level rise and climate change. Whereas human settlement and inhabitation in these locations initially co-existed in a much more symbiotic relationship with their natural landscapes and ecologies, the natural geography of this territory writ-large has been significantly impacted and altered by a manufactured landscape. Design strategies can also build on new modes of design representation, employing mapping as a process of design research.

The competition brief challenged designers to develop schemes addressing the perceived failings of the post war American city, offering solutions for the vacancies from previous failed urban renewal programs, and the ensuing urban decay and flight from the city. Perhaps, most importantly, is the ability of design to act in a milieu not possessing the political will or agency to address the pressing issues of sea-level rise and climate change in coastal cities. The schemes should offer design strategies, which lie in more symbiotic relationships between city and nature, including the Hillsborough River and the Tampa Bay and its estuary. It should be noted, however, that recent trends currently show, in fact, the population to be actually increasing as migration flows of the Baby Boomer retirement generation move to Sunbelt coastal cities seeking warmer climates and cheaper housing prices than those available in the North.

THE COMPETITION

The competition had both national, as well as international participation, bringing forth the best practices for designing for resiliency in coastal cities from all over the world. The invited jurors, prominent theorists as well as practitioners in urban design and landscape urbanism - Margaret Crawford, Juhani Pallasmaa, Chad Oppenheim, Chris Reed and Charles Waldheim - discussed the opportunities for the envisioning, as well as the re-thinking of these urban landscapes.

Juror Charles Waldheim lectured broadly about the agency that the Design Ideas Competition possesses, and the pivotal role that it continues to play in re-defining urban design and theory, citing such seminal examples as the competition for the Parc de la Villette in Paris' nineteenth arrondissement, a former slaughterhouse. Both Bernard Tschumi's project, as well as the OMA scheme for Parc de la Villette, reconsidered the re-programming of the urban condition through the programming of the landscape of a thickened surface, as well as the juxtaposition of programmatic bands with indeterminate and flexible programs. As Waldheim discussed, more recent design competitions, such as that of the Downsview Park competition, an international competition for an urban park design for a former military base in Toronto, Canada, have focused on the integration of ecologies and habitat into design schemes. So did the naturalization of the Mouth of the Don competition, also located in Toronto. Here, the previous infrastructure of the Don River was softened and re-naturalized at its mouth where it empties out into Lake Ontario, thus creating an urban estuary, as well as catalyzing a re-thinking of the co-existing natural habitat with landscape systems.

THE COMPETITION SCHEMES

Many of the competition schemes featured here investigate resiliency as a design strategy. The winning schemes distinguished themselves by addressing the issues of the competition framework, including landscape recovery. in addition to the contemporary urban issues in the post-war Coastal American city such as designing with vacancies. This also included the de-engineering of infrastructures from the failed paradigms of post-war city planning policies, at the same time as layering resiliencies and ecologies into strategic planning and frameworks. The competition entries, which are featured here, are analyzed and considered for their contribution to new and more flexible frameworks of urban design and planning design for the Post-War Coastal American city through Ecologies. The winning schemes for (Re)stitch Tampa distinguish themselves by challenging existing planning norms through ecological urbanism. Schemes also examine alternative methods of representation and process in urban design. The featured schemes address the city through the three mutually reinforcing lenses, which framed the competition, those of *ecology, infrastructure* and *connectivity*. Landscape infrastructure becomes the underling structure and connective tissue of the urban system. The schemes also critique the single-use zoning, of the Modernist, post-war city.

WINNING SCHEMES

1. Flowscape. Visions for a New Urban Estuary proposes the de-engineering and re-programming of the previous regimes of historic infrastructures, resulting from poor-sighted urban policy decisions. Its underlying concepts propose the re-calibration of the historically oppositional relationships between land and water, in addition to critiquing the previous regimes of decades-old infrastructural projects and their resulting fragmentation of cities. It also proposes the reclaiming, as well as the re-assigning of new and layered programs between the interface of the city and the water.

The scheme introduces an urban bayou along the underside of the Crosstown Expressway along its right of way. It affords a large-scale re-stitch in a swapping out of parking on the land for an ecological system. Thus, the bayou is connected to the Tampa Bay natural estuary, the city, and the Shipping Channel. Here, design strategies engage ecological processes in their frameworks. This scheme creates urban marshlands that integrate liquid programs into the city, as well as integrating both urban, and ecological relationships within the city. This scheme re-organizes and aggregates the surface, re-stitching the forgotten layers of the city, creating a layering of programs, as well as new flows and movements. Soft-infrastructure can accommodate flooding.

The strategies used here address the disinvestment of the public realm, as well as integrating flood protection onto the city grid and its systems.

2. (re) stitch (re)silience is an elegant design strategy which pays homage to the intrinsic relationship and symbiotic siting of the initial human settlement in the region with respect to its fragile eco-systems and their natural resources. The design's overarching intent is to make the city more resilient to sea level rise, in addition to creating a public water space in the River which registers the changing water levels.

An archipelago design strategy addresses the current vacancies in the urban fabric, which are aggregated through the recovering and reclaiming of the landscape. A floating public square acts both as a public space and as a scaffolding for layered programs and ecological services. It also acts as storage for storm water and purification systems. PARK in lots re-introduce layered programs, which engage both the water, as well as the integration of urban and ecological systems and the transformation of infrastructures. It creates different matrices of green infrastructure, in addition to re-naturalizing the post-war coastal city.

3. Stitches Fabrics, another winning scheme featured here, offers a proposal for not only a singular scheme, yet for a number of possible different scenarios, which are flexible, operating within the framework of the post-war coastal American city. Schemes plan for a shifting landscape, through both flexible, as well as indeterminate programs, where design has the agency to address uncertainties. The proposal identifies points for individual stitching to occur. These stitches, when aggregated or combined, have the agency to become activated as part of a larger, scalar proposal. In their overall totality, they have the agency to activate new programs within the city. Strategies include those of infill, as well as the introduction of tidal zones and aquatic typologies within the city grid. The scheme reclaims infrastructure for other uses, introducing layered programs within these substrates.

HONORABLE MENTIONS

1. Pleating Tampa takes a spatial approach from that of the fabric analogy from re-stitching, by introducing a series of spatial operations based on "the pleat", and how this might relate to its layered ecological functions. The scheme identifies four layers, which are focused as areas for focal pleats, which create a layering of activities. It underlines the agency of ecology to transform and reshape the city, by the intensification of programs, as well as the re-envisioning of infrastructures and ecologies.

The pleat is an analogy to the stitch, which becomes the area for engagement where the infrastructure is spatially operated on through the pleat intervention, and where the overlaying of ecological infrastructures become new substrates and scaffoldings for multi-layered and multi-programmed surfaces. The spatial operation of the pleat creates both transitions, as well as habitats with local ecologies. The typology of the pleat, as well as the scaffolding and the spatial focusing, is a similar strategy but different to that of another scheme, the Eco Grid. The Eco Grid proposes the superimposition of an ecological grid onto that of the gridded generic American city, which is irrespective of natural geographies and ecologies.

2. Rehydrate Tampa proposes an overlay of ecological systems and infrastructures. These create new armatures for the city, in addition to investigating and reconstructing the current land-water edge condition, proposing the transformation of the hard infrastructures into performative soft infrastructures. This strategy re-choreographs the ebbs and the flows of the city, in order to repair and recover the landscape, while addressing the current nitrogen loading and algae blooms that are impacting it. It focuses on performative water systems, proposing a framework of "plumbing" strategies. These are integrated into the neighborhood building typologies, as well as overlaying and blurring the grid, thus creating new spatial conditions for the post-war coastal city. New micro-industries are created, which serve to replace the obsolete and abandoned former post-industrial industries. These include street interventions, as well as the integration of flooding design strategies. The scheme, like many others, challenge the prevailing urban renewal decisions still omni-present within the city, with its heavy-handed infrastructure and its unintended consequences including the fragmentation and the disconnection of the urban fabric to the River.

3. Re-stitch Tampa.The Sub-urban Mix is one of the few schemes that addresses the reconnection of the outlying suburbs - where, in fact, 80% of Tampa's population currently live - back to the city. The scheme activates the middle landscape which lies in between - the former trolley suburbs and vacant, interstitial lands. It insightfully critiques the post-war city's characteristic single-use zoning. The scheme introduces a larger, regional scale back into the city, connecting the post-war suburbs through meaningful ecological networks, as opposed to solely by highway infrastructure and vehicular transportation. It also overlays the possibilities of alternative methods of transportation onto them. The scheme identifies the River as the geographic center and the new spine for the city, while re-introducing ecologies and new programs as well as new systems along the river, making it culturally meaningful. It densifies the aggregated vacancies on the West side of the Hillsborough River within the city, opposite the northern anchor of the Riverwalk. These areas were subject to the urban renewal clearance projects in Tampa during the 1960ies and never fully rebuilt.

4. Shifting Currents designs with water urbanisms, with the premise that they have the potential to be transformative for the city. Similar to (**re**) **stitch Resilience,** this scheme engages the tactic of an island and archipelago design strategy. This creates an urban shift and is speculative with the introduction of tidal zones that which act as catalysts for the intensification of a more fluid and ecological relationship between urban functions. These create resiliency and a foundation for projected future growth and development. It introduces natural water, blurring the edges and boundaries with a layering of biodiversity. It designs around the framework of flooding changes, proposing the flooding of underdeveloped and underutilized parking lots for wetland restoration. While such schemes might suggest erasure, it is projected that they actually serve to increase land-value, while at the same time as creating water-based transportation and layered land-water uses and programs throughout the city.

5. Symbiosis Ri-verizing Tampa as with other schemes, is also one of inversion, which seeks to strengthen the relationship between the city and the River, as opposed to polarizing the relationship between the two, a fundamental tenet of the competition. As in many of the schemes, ecology acts as a placeholder for both a sustainable system of storm water management, which can integrate sea level rise strategies, at the same time as providing a placeholder for recreation and programming. This scheme was appreciated by local jurors for its sensitivity to local Tampa issues in its programming.

ADDITIONAL SELECTED PROPOSALS

1. Streets. Branches of the River proposal literally stretches water tributaries, from the Hillsborough River into the city, replacing streets, thus becoming the conceptual branches or tributaries of the river overlaid onto the city. The scheme locates strategic points within the land-water interface of the city, at the same time as addressing an overlay strategy of constructed wetlands in the vacancies. It also serves as an overlay of the urban watershed. It integrates best practices in storm water management, with its constructing of hydrological systems, and the overlay of these onto the city grid with green and blue corridors that function as new street systems. This has the effect of introducing new kinds of ebbs flows throughout the city, while strengthening the connection to its warterfront.

2. Tampa (Eco) Grid overarching spatial operation is one of an eco-grid overlaid onto the generic postwar city grid, which is predominantly irrespective of the terrain's natural topography and geography. The scheme proposes the transformation of the city from one of urban fragmentation and disconnection to new urban public spaces. The River is perceived as a new geographic connector for disconnected programs, activities and districts. Programs create infrastructures with local ecologies, and the highway infrastructure becomes a new substrate and scaffolding for local ecologies, as well as a new platform infrastructure for programs and new ways of experiencing the city.

3. Spur On / Spur Off Ecology / Infrastructure / Connectivity + Economy critiques the function or lack of function of the off-ramp infrastructure of the I275 into downtown Tampa, which currently connects to Ashley Street from the north. It explores the possibilities nascent in the in-between spaces that it is currently occupying. In Tampa's case, these were several vibrant neighborhoods, which were "taken" during urban renewal. The infrastructure, in a sense, creates the boundaries and the gaps in-between the neighborhood fabric. Unlike the other schemes featured, it proposes a large "big urban project" which both provokes as well as challenges the competition framework. It also combines ecological remediation, while layering different urban events within the Big Urban Project of the stadium that it proposes.

4. The Spine as with many of the schemes, and in keeping with the overarching framework of the design competition, advocates for a more symbiotic relationship between the city and the river through softening the currently oppositional relationship identified between the two in Tampa. The engagement of ecology as active and dynamic, distinguishes itself in this scheme from not simply acting as a placeholder. This scheme comprises a clever, overarching spatial solution where remediation plays an active role. This remediation aspect of the project drives the scheme by making a significant attempt to bring back the once robust ecologies of the river, and, at the same time, creating new and layered programs which choreograph the circulation and experiential qualities of the city vis-à-vis its re-found ecologies.

5. Reclaim Tampa offers new typologies, design guidelines as well as best practices for stormwater management, overlaid with their potential to become new civic infrastructure, layered with place making. The scheme engages the concept of phasing over time, as well as urban incremental design, with its proposal to decommission the street system, as well as other city systems and the possible return of them to nature. Ecology thus becomes a productive landscape for the city. Aquaculture, as an economy based on local ecologies, is introduced. The scheme is also multi-scalar, reconnecting the landscape, as well as both reclaiming and creating microclimates using native plants. The premise is that these function not just as aesthetic landscapes, yet also as systems, with the agency to become integrated into functioning storm-water management infrastructure.

CONCLUSIONS

(Re) Stitch Tampa, as a research platform, fundamentally questions the prevailing frameworks and methods of traditional urban design practices. It also challenges traditional city planning strategies, which design cities through a weightier approach of buildings, which also employ single-use zoning. The schemes featured here and resulting from the competition, reintroduce the River as the new spine and lifeline of the city, while creating new and layered programs along it. This resonates with design strategies of flexibility and open-endedness for programming. It also integrates performative design aspects through a re-working of the river's infrastructure. It begins with a new spine for the city, as well as the re-introduction of new ecologies which re-connect the city to the water.

The projects emerging from the (Re) Stitch Tampa project have the potential to have a life beyond the competition itself. They offer a tool-kit of possible design strategies for architects, planners and city planning agencies, as well as the constituents, stakeholders and developers, vis-à-vis public place-making in the post-war coastal American city. This publication should be used as both a toolkit, as well as a handbook which affords an alternative insight for both designing, as well as recovering cities and their landscapes. These include tactical strategies, designing for resiliency, flexibilities, which engage multiple readings and possibilities.

As initiated by the competition brief, connective urban landscapes and ecological infrastructure have the agency to function as the underlying framework. The featured schemes here robustly address the competition charge, designing frameworks with ecologies, as opposed to a singular proposal. Within this framework, these strategies can act as catalysts for the economic redevelopment of the city, in addition to calibrating the reconnection of the city to its nature, while ameliorating its current fragmentation.

Other notable coastal cities in Florida, such as Port Charlotte, south of Tampa, have adopted more progressive design strategies for their land-water edges, which might also serve as useful precedents. After Hurricane Charley in 2004 severely impacted Port Charlotte, the city engaged a strategy of acquiring land through rolling coastal easements, land banking and compensating those property owners with the properties impacted. The vacated land became part of a public trust for the city of parklands and areas for coastal replenishment, and building for resiliency. As a strategy, the design is more flexible and that allows the city to replenish their valuable wetlands, which can mitigate storm surge.

In a milieu where there does not exist the robust political will to address these increasingly critical issues facing Florida's coastal cities, as well as other coastal cities within North America and the world, it is the charge of designers, trained in stewardship, who must be tactical in their design gestures and strategies, with an overarching agenda for the greater public realm.

EPILOGUE-DIY (DO IT YOURSELF) (RE) STITCH TAMPA

There were a number of significant public space projects which were actually implemented shortly after the (re) stitch Tampa awards ceremony on April 12, 2012. The city received a significant TIGER (Transportation Investment Generating Economic Recovery) federal grant, which in part was used to finish the remaining segment of the Tampa Riverwalk, which has recently just opened. Additionally, a green pedestrian right of way is being implemented along the right of way under the Crosstown Expressway. The abandoned Waterworks Park industrial building on the northern anchor parcel of the Riverwalk was adaptively re-used as a restaurant, and the natural spring there as well as a city park. Ulele Spring was recovered and connected to the River, in addition to undergoing a significant shore-softening strategy and habitat restoration. Its warmer water temperatures serve as a destination for the manatee, which swim up the Hillsborough River from the Tampa Bay Estuary into the downtown core.

Perhaps most inspiring is The Tampa Green Artery project, a grassroots, bottom-up organization with a mission to complete a 22-mile planned, perimeter trail throughout Tampa. Through the aggregation of vacancies and other opportunities, this dedicated group continues to connect the neighborhoods of Tampa and various public spaces with off-water and close to water trails.

1   Gary R. Mormino, "WPA in Florida", FORUM (The Magazine of the Florida Humanities Council), Issue 25-Nov./Dec. 2005.

2   Empirical observation of the author.

3   "Manuel Leto, Cigar City Magazine.

The Sensuous City

Reflections on the Poetics of Urban Experience

Juhani Pallasmaa

Architect, Professor (Helsinki)

"In the fusion of place and soul, the soul is as much of a container of place as place is a container of soul, and both are susceptible to the same forces of destruction."[1]
Robert Pogue Harrison

CITY AS A MENTAL INSTRUMENT

We tend to think of cities merely as material and utilitarian structures. Yet, the city, even more than the house, is also an instrument of existential and metaphysical significance, an intricate device that structures hierarchy and action, mobility and exchange, societal organization and cultural symbolization, identity and memory. Undoubtedly, the most significant and complex of human artifacts, it controls and entices, symbolizes and represents, expresses and conceals. Cities and settlements are the most significant witnesses of the course of cultural evolution. Human settlements are inhabited excavations of the archeology of culture, and they expose the dense fabric of societal and individual life, both past and present. A city always contains more than can be described. It is an endless generator of images and experiences, situations and encounters, harmonies and discords. Simultaneously a maze of clarity and opacity, the city exhausts the capacity of human description and imagination: disorder plays against order, accidental against the regular, and surprise against the anticipated. Activities and functions interpenetrate and rub against each other creating contradictions, paradoxes, and an excitement of an erotic nature.

In *Invisible Cities*, Italo Calvino describes the mental peculiarities of over fifty imaginary cities, and expands thus essentially the number of cities known by geographers. For him, the city is a memory device, similar to the secret devices of the great orators of Antiquity, who placed the various parts of their speech in spaces and places of an imagined building, to be retrieved and re-membered in proper order when delivering the speech. Calvino describes the City of Zora, "a city that no one, having seen it, can forget":

46

"This city which cannot be expunged from the mind is like an armature, a honeycomb in whose cells each of us can place the things he wants to remember: names of famous men, virtues, numbers, vegetable and mineral classifications, dates of battles, constellations, parts of speech. Between each idea and each point of the itinerary an affinity or a contrast can be established, serving as an immediate aid to memory. So the world's most learned men are those who have memorized Zora."[2]

Also real places and cities concretize and reinforce our recollection of events and persons. We live in cities of the mind that are real and fictional, objective and of our own imaginative making, at the same time.

THE CITY OF THE EYE

The contemporary city is the city of the eye. Rapid mechanized movement detaches us from a bodily and intimate contact with urban space. As the city of the gaze passivates the body and the other senses, the alienation of the body further reinforces the role of vision. The passivation of the body gives rise to a condition that is similar to the dulled consciousness induced by television; we turn from active participants into passive onlookers and bodiless spectators.

Cartesian and perspectival, the modern city has gradually eliminated the specificity of place and detached verticality from horizontality. Instead of joining seamlessly to give rise to a plasticity and unity of the landscape, these two dimensions have become separate projections; the plan has been detached from the section. Also the structure of the city is detached from real patterns of spontaneous behavior, movement, and life. The modern visual city leaves us as outsiders, voyeuristic spectators and momentary visitors, incapable of true participation and identification.

Visual alienation has been further reinforced by the inventions of photography and the printed image, which have created an ever-expanding Sargasso Sea of images. The camera has become the prime instrument of tourism. "The omnipresence of photographs has an incalculable effect on our ethical sensibility," writes Susan Sontag, describing a "mentality that looks at the world

as a set of potential photographs."[3] As a consequence, "[R]eality has come to seem more and more like what we are shown by cameras", she observes, and assumes that "taking photographs has set up a chronic voyeuristic relation to the world which levels the meaning of all events."[4] Indeed, we can easily catch ourselves looking at a scene unconsciously framed as a photographic image; the tourist's city is a collection of pre-selected visual pictures instead of lived embodied experiences. The increasing use of mirrored glass, surfaces that return our gaze back to us without affect or knowledge of life behind the surreal surfaces, contributes to the experience of superficial flatness, as opposed to that of depth, opacity and mystery. Today's city of transparency and reflection has lost its materiality, depth, and shadow. We need secrecy and shadow as urgently as we desire to see and to know; the visible and the invisible, the known and what is beyond knowledge, have to obtain a balance. Our consciousness as well as neural and perceptual systems are actively searching mechanisms, which become frustrated by only perceiving the self-evident. Opacity and secrecy feed imagination and make one imagine life behind the city's surfaces and walls. The obsessively functionalized city of the age of rationality has turned too readily legible, too evident, leaving no opportunity for mystery, fantasy and dreaming. As the city loses its haptic intimacy, secrecy and invitation, it loses its sensuality, erotic charge and invitation.

THE HAPTIC CITY

The haptic city welcomes us as citizens, fully authorized to participate in its daily life. It creates a sense of intimacy and belonging, evoking our sense of empathy and engaging our emotions.

The experience of the pleasurable city is not a visual image, but an embodied percept based on a peculiar double fusion: we inhabit the city, and the city dwells in us. When entering a new city, we immediately begin to accommodate ourselves in its structures and cavities, and the city begins to inhabit us. As the French poet Noël Arnaud suggests: "I am the space, where I am".[5] All the cities that we have ever visited have become part of our identity and consciousness.

1

When describing how a traveler is able to identify the various types of buildings – the palace, the barracks, the mill, the theatre, the bazaar - in the City of Zoe, Calvino states: "This ... confirms the hypothesis that each man bears in his mind a city made only of differences, a city without figures and without forms, and the individual cities fill it up."[6] In the same way that we carry the archetypal image of the room, the house and the home since our early childhood, we also possess a mental image of the city, which we re-adjust to the varying conditions of reality.

The mental experience and memory of the city is more an embodied and haptic constellation than a sequence of visual images; impressions of sight are embedded in the continuum of unconscious haptic experiences. Even as the eye touches and the gaze strokes distant outlines and contours, our vision *feels* the hardness, texture, weight, moistness and temperature of the surfaces. Without the collaboration of touch, the eye would even be unable to decipher space and depth, and we could not mould the mosaic of sensory impressions into a coherent and plastic continuum. The experience of embodied continuity unites isolated sensory fragments in the temporal continuum of the sense of self.

In addition to our five Aristotelian senses, we have an atmospheric sense that grasps immediately the character of complex settings, before we have had any time to consciously observe or analyze its features or qualities. This comprehensive atmospheric sense, could well be regarded as our sixth and most important sense. Besides, the senses constantly collaborate, interact and interfuse, evoking thus a full existential experience and sense of being, which is a totally different quality than the mere additive result of our five senses.

"My perception is [therefore] not a sum of visual, tactile, and audible givens: I perceive in a total way with my whole being; I grasp a unique structure of the thing, a unique way of being, which speaks to all my senses at once," as Merleau-Ponty writes emphatically.[7]

In his essay "Eye and Mind", Merleau-Ponty makes a significant remark on embodiment in the art of painting: "Quality, light, color, depth, which are there before us, are there only because they awaken an echo in our body and because the body welcomes them [...] Things have an internal equivalence in me; they arouse in me a carnal formula of their presence."[8] This "carnal formula" gives the works of art and architecture their very sense of life. A profound piece of art, architecture, or urban setting, evokes a sense of life, and this quality usually projects epic experiences.

Thus, I confront the city with my entire body; my legs measure the length of the arcade and the width of the square; my gaze unconsciously projects my body on the façades of buildings, where it roams imaginatively on the cornices and contours, groping for the size of recesses and projections; my body weight meets the mass of the door, and my hand grasps the door pull, polished to a sheen by countless generations, as I enter the dark void behind. The city and the body supplement each other; they mutually define each other. The city is a true extension of my body and mind, and the city has its second, immaterial life in my recollections, fantasies, and dreams.

HEARING THE CITY, CITY OF THE BODY

The final chapter of Steen Eiler Rasmussen's perceptive book, *Experiencing Architecture,* is significantly entitled

"Hearing Architecture."[9] No doubt, every city has its specific soundscape and echo, depending on the scale and pattern of its streets, as well as on its dominant architectural styles and materials. The most intimate encounter with any city is hearing the echo of one's own footsteps. The ears scan the boundaries of space, and determine its scale, shape and materiality; the ears caress the walls. Rasmussen even recalls the architecture of the echo in the underground tunnels of Vienna in Carol Reed's film *The Third Man*, starring Orson Welles: "Your ear receives the impact of both the length and the cylindrical form of the tunnel."[10]

In fact, recent scholarship suggests that early architectural spaces were conceived more for their acoustic properties, than visual qualities. "When architectural historians begin to realize that most ancient buildings were constructed not so much to enclose space, as to enshrine sound, a new era of the subject will open out."[11]

Parks and squares silence the deafening rumble of the city, allowing us to hear the ripple of water and the twitter of birds. A park creates an oasis in the urban desert, enabling us to sense the fragrance of flowers, the moistness of morning dew, and the sweet smell of newly cut grass. Parks permit us to be simultaneously surrounded by the city, and to be outside of it. They are metaphors of the absence of the city, but at the same time, parks are minia-turized still lifes, and images of constructed nature and Paradise; the word paradise actually derives from the ancient Persian word, *pairidaeza,* which means "walled garden". Paradoxically, paradise seems to be an urban dream rather than of nature *in-statu-nascendi.*

The power of hearing in creating a sensation of space, can be immediate and unexpected; waking up to the sound of an ambulance in a nocturnal city, we instantly reconstruct our identity and location. Before falling back to solitary slumber, we become aware of the immensity of the sleeping city, with its countless dreaming inhabitants in the manner that the protagonist of Marcel Proust's, *In Search of Lost Time,* gradually reconstructs his identity and location:

[M]y sleep was so heavy ... then I lost all sense of the place in which I had gone to sleep, and when I awoke in the middle of the night, not knowing where I was, I could not even be sure at first who I was; I had only the most rudimentary sense of existence ... My body, still too heavy with sleep to move, would endeavor to construe from the pattern of its tiredness the position of its various limbs, in order to deduce there from the direction of the wall, the location of the furniture, to piece together and give a name to the house in which it lay. Its memory, the composite memory of its ribs, its knees, its shoulder-blades, offered it a series of rooms in which it had at one time or another slept, while the unseen walls, shift-ing and adapting themselves to the shape of each successive room that it remembered, whirled round it in the dark.[12]

Proust's literary description makes the reader fully grasp the embodied essence of memory, and indeed, recent psychological investigations suggest that we could not perceive anything without the interplay of our sense systems with memory and imagination. "We could not see light without our inner light", Arthur Zajonc, the physicist, argues.[13]

We grasp the city as an embodied experience; its structure and grain are as much haptic experiences of the body as retinal images of vision, and I feel my city primarily as a body image. My intestines memorize the city I live in, and I orient myself by means of this internalized compass more than by a mental map or mere vision. My hometown is as much an image of my bowels as of the conscious intellect.

Vittorio Gallese, one of the two discoverers of the mirror neurons, argues: "Sympathy is an unconscious process in which the individual uses his own body as a template that enables him to 'feel' into the other's experience".[14] We do not only share the feelings of other human beings, as we are also capable of feeling the weight, hardness, texture, temperature and moisture of matter. Through our capacities of embodiment, empathy, memory and imagination, we live in a live world, which is articulated and poeticised by profound architecture. Due to this experience of a distinct life force, artistic and architectural works are born and experienced in an animistic manner. Profound architecture speaks to us, guides our movements and caresses our body and skin. "Have you not noticed, in walking about the city, that among the buildings with which it is peopled, certain are *mute*; others *speak*; and, others, finally – and they are the most rare – *sing*?", Paul Valéry suggests.[15] "Poeticization" of architecture implies the re-identification of the mythic and archetypal echoes of the primordial buildings in our collective memory, as well as the mental equivalents of physical objects and properties hidden in our deep memory.

CIITY AND WATER

All cities located by water are fortunate; the encounter of man-made stonewalls and water is entirely metaphysical. In the words of Adrian Stokes, the British painter and art essayist, "The hesitancy of water reveals architectural immobility."[16] Cities which are located by the water – the shore of an ocean, river or lake, or a maze of man-made canals – are lucky as the liveliness and playfulness of water create a fundamental contrast to the silent immobility of the stacked stones of the city. Water provides a mirror for the city to double its life and beauty, and water is an invitation to the imagina-

tion. Water always evokes distances, images of otherness, and it creates a state of dreaming and journey. No wonder in Italo Calvino's *The Invisible Cities,* Marco Polo tells Kublai Khan about countless dream cities of imagination, which all end up being descriptions of Venice, the traveller's home town.

The inherent cosmopolitanism of harbors, and their juxtaposition of images of permanence and motion, stability and journey, ignite fantasies and dreaming. The smell of seaweed, and the shrill cries of seagulls, make one think of the depths of the oceans, of distant lands and exotic customs, of the excitement of travel and the sweet longing for home. As Joseph Brodsky observes: "The more one travels, the more complex one's sense of nostalgia becomes."[17]

Cities without the soothing presence of water usually appear thirsty and breathless. Even an occasional rivulet, pond or fountain, provides an escape from this urban thirst and mental need to experience the lively mobility and reflections of water. As Gaston Bachelard writes, water is the most powerfully poeticizing of all elements; he writes appropriately of "water poets."[18] In his view, water is a feminine element, but when it rushes forcefully, it obtains a masculine character. Water is also suggestive of both life and death, and these multiple and conflicting associations help to explain the forceful impact of water on our imagination.

In *Watermark*, his poetic book on Venice, Joseph Brodsky repeatedly equates time and water, stating: "I simply think that water is the image of time."[19] The poet is right. Water possesses the liquidity of time, as well as its alternating transparency and opacity. Water flows rapidly or slowly, and its final destination is unavoidable; both time and water approach death, a final equilibrium in immobility, "the horizontal death" suggested by Bachelard.[20] No wonder water, the double of time and beauty, is so important for architecture.

Brodsky gives a lively description of his native water city, St. Petersburg, on the River Neva:

The twelve-mile long Neva, branching right in the center of town, with its twenty-five large and small coiling canals, provides this city with such a quantity of

1. Panorama of Tampa's Post-Industrial Waterfront with Tampa Armature Worksand Trolley Barn-Softened Ecological Edge Returning Back to the Natural Landscape.
2. CAMLS–Center for Advanced Learnings and Medical Simulation, USF, Venue for Final Competition Exhibit andAwards Ceremony for (Re) Stitch Tampa.

mirrors, that narcissism becomes inevitable. Reflected every second by thousands of square feet of running silver amalgam, it's as if the city were constantly being filmed by its river ... on a sunny day, [it] looks like a depository of these blinding images. No wonder that sometimes this city gives the impression of an utter egoist preoccupied solely with its own appearance ... The inexhaustible, maddening multiplication of all these pilasters, colonnades, porticoes hints at the nature of this urban narcissism, hints at the possibility that at least in the inanimate world, water may be regarded as a condensed form of time.[21]

This could well be a literary description of the river front in Tampa, Florida.

CITY AS A COLLAGE

There is hardly any city in the entire world that would have been conceived and built as a singular coherent entity, as cities are unavoidably a result of gradual growth and repeated changes under varying cultural, economic and technological conditions, as well as of a continuous process of demolishing and rebuilding. The city is the art form of collage and cinematic montage *par excellence*; we experience it as an endless juxtaposition of themes, motives and impressions. Collage and montage are the most characteristic artistic strategies of the modern and postmodern eras. The contemporary

interest in collage reflects a fascination for fragments and discontinuities, and a nostalgia for traces of time. The incredible acceleration of speed - of movement, information, and images - has collapsed time onto the flat screen of the present, upon which the simultaneity of the world is projected. As time loses its duration, depth, and echo in the past, man loses his sense of self as a historical being, and is threatened by the shadows of the past. "Long novels written today are perhaps a contradiction," writes Italo Calvino and continues: "The dimension of time has been shattered, we cannot live or think except in fragments of time, each of which goes off along its own trajectory and immediately disappears. We can rediscover the continuity of time only in the novels of that period when time no longer seemed stopped and did not yet seem to have exploded..."[22]

The city's structures capture, slow down, and preserve time in the same way as literary and other artistic works. Buildings, streets, and squares enable us to return back to the past, to times before our own birth, and to experience the slow and healing presence of past time. The greatest of architectural monuments are museums of time that halt and suspend time for eternity. Buildings of the past are also stores and containers of silence; great buildings of the past enable us to experience the silence before our mechanized, accelerated, and obsessive time.

URBAN IMAGINATION

We cannot mentally live in a non-place, and thus we always domesticate our limitless and anonymous world by turning it into a sequence of distinct places. We have an innate capacity for remembering and imagining places; without this merciful shell of memory and fantasy, we would be forever homeless. Perception, memory, and imagination, are in constant inter-action; the domain of our present is merged with images of memory and fantasy; memory penetrates into imagination. We continually construct an immense city of evocation and remembrance, and all the cities we have visited are precincts in this fictitious metropolis of the mind.

Literature and cinema would be devoid of their enchantment, without our capacity to enter a remembered or imagined place. Memory returns us to distant places, and novels transport us through cities invoked by the magic of the writer's words. The rooms, squares, and streets portrayed by a great writer are as vivid as any space that we have actually visited. The city of San Francisco unfolds in its multiplicity through the montage of Alfred Hitch-cock's *Vertigo*; we enter the haunting edifices in the steps of the protago-nist, and see them through his eyes. We become citizens of St. Petersburg through the incantation of Fjodor Dostoyevsky; we step into the room of Raskolnikov's shocking double murder, and we are one of the terrified spec-tators watching Mikolka and his drunken friends beat a horse to death on a side street of St. Petersburg; we feel genuinely frustrated at our inability to prevent this insane and purposeless cruelty. Our most important ethical lessons, are the ones offered to our imaginative judgment by great writers and artists.

There is, however, a difference between cities as visited and as imagined; the intangible cities of imagination cannot be remembered in detail, they fade away immediately as the dream drifts away, and they can only be con-jured back by the magical words of the writer. That is why great books have to be re-read, great paintings re-viewed, and great buildings re-visited. There are cities that remain mere distant visual images when remembered, and cities that are remembered in all their vivacity. Memory re-evokes the delightful city with all its sounds and smells, and its changing lights and shadows. I can even choose whether to walk on the sunny or the shaded side of the street, in the pleasurable city of my remembrance.

The measure of the sense of the city is this: can you hear the laughter of children, the flutter of pigeon wings, and the shouting of the peddler in the city of your memory? Can you recall the echo of your own footsteps in the city of your mind? Can you imagine yourself falling in love in that city?

"It is as though space, cognizant … of its inferiority to time, answers it with the only property time doesn't possess: with beauty".
Joseph Brodsky

1   Robert Pogue Harrison, "Sympathetic Miracles", *Gardens: An Essay on the Human Condition*, The University of Chicago Press, Chicago and London, p. 130.

2   Italo Calvino, *Invisible Cities*, Pan Book Ltd., London, 1979, pp. 16-17.

3   Susan Sontag, *On Photography*, Penguin Books, New York, 1986, p. 24.

4   Sontag, ibid., pp. 11 and 16.

5   As quoted in Gaston Bachelard, The Poetics of Space, Beacon Press, Boston, 1969, p. 137.

6   Calvino, op. cit., p. 29.

7   Maurice Merleau-Ponty, "The Film and the New Pscyhology", *Sense and Non-Sense,* North western University Press, Evanston, IL, 1964, p. 50.

8   As quoted in Charles Tomlinson, "The poet as painter", in J.M. McClatchy, ed., *Poets on Painters*, University of California Press, Berkeley, Los Angeles and London, 1990, p. 275.

9   Steen Eiler Rasmussen, *Experiencing Architecture*, The MIT Press, March, 1964.

10   Rasmussen, op. cit., p. 225.

11   Murray Schafer in the 1970s, as referred to in Professor Sarah Robinson's letter to the writer, 20 March, 2012.

12   Marcel Proust, *In Search of Lost Time, Volume 1: Swann's Way*, Vintage/Random House Inc., London, 1996, p. 4.

13   Arthur Zajonc, *Catching the Light: The Entwined History of Light and Mind*, Oxford University Press, New York, 1995, p. 5.

14   As quoted in Arnold H. Modell, *Imagination and the Meaningful Brain*, The MIT Press, Cambridge, Massachusetts, 2006, p. 121.

15   Paul Valéry, "Eupalinos, or the Architect", *Dialogues*, Pantheon Books, New York, 1956, p. 83.

16   Adrian Stokes, "Prologue: at Venice", *The Critical Writings of Adrian Stokes*, vol. II, Thames and Hudson, Plymouth, 1978, p. 88.

17   Joseph Brodsky, "A Place as Good as Any", in *On Grief and Reason*, Farrar, Straus and Giroux, New York, 1997, p. 35.

18   Gaston Bachelard, *Water and Dreams: An Essay on the Imagination of Matter*, The Pegasus Foundation, Dallas, Texas, 1983, p. 5.

19   Joseph Brodsky, *Watermark*, Penguin Books, London, 1992, p. 44.

20   Gaston Bachelard, *Water and Dreams: An Essay on the Imagination of Matter*, The Pegasus Foundation, Dallas, Texas, 1983.

21   Joseph Brodsky, "A Guide to a Renamed City", *Less Than One: Selected Essays*, Farrar Straus Giroux, New York, 1986, p. 77.

22   Italo Calvino, *If on a winter's night a traveller*, Harcourt Brace & Company, Orlando, FL, 1979, p. 8.

23   Joseph Brodsky, *Watermark*, Penguin Books, London, p. 44.

Winning Schemes

Flowscape

Vision for a New Urban Estuary

Group Han Associates-Michael Chaveriat, Yikyu Choe, Myung Kweon Park

New York City, NY, USA

Legend

1. TECO Trolley Barn Live/Work Lofts
2. University of Tampa
3. Blake High School
4. Performing Arts Center
5. Tampa Museum of Art
6. Curtis Hixon Park
7. Kiley Gardens
8. Tampa Theatre
9. Nature's Classroom Downtown
10. Tampa Convention Center
11. Tampa General Hospital
12. Florida Aquarium
13. Pineland Ecology park and playground
14. Tampa Thunderdome
15. Cotanchobee Park

Water

Ecology

Storm Water

Flood Protection

FLOWSCAPE

Movement

People

Wildlife

Water

Nutrients

City

Culture

Commerce

Parks

Transit

Tampa Heights

Cultural District

⑧

⑤

⑥

⑦

②

Downtown Bayou

⑬

Channel District

⑫

⑭

⑨

Gateway District

⑩

⑪

Harbour Island

0   500   1000

The city of Tampa has always been defined by its relationship to the water. Over the decades, this relationship has taken many forms. In 1891, Henry Plant established his iconic Tampa Bay Hotel on the shores of the Hillsborough River when it was still considered to be romantic and wild. More recently, Tampa has been characterized by an oppositional relationship between the built city and the water. The once integrated ecosystem was progressively segregated from the city over the past several decades. With a hard-edged engineered shoreline and neglected riverfront sites, it seemed as though the city turned its back to the water. Now, major efforts are being made to re-establish this vital relationship. A more continuous Riverwalk is under construction, shore softening is taking place, and large parks and cultural institutions are finding a new life along the water. Taking this positive trajectory into account, how can we think beyond the water's edge and imagine the rivers, channels and bay as catalysts for change?

Similar to its riverfront, Tampa's urban core suffers from problems caused by decades old infrastructure projects. Downtown Tampa is fragmented by the heavy infrastructure that facilitates the driving culture of the city, and its surrounding suburbs. The Lee Roy Selmon Crosstown Expressway runs through the heart of the city, effectively splitting it into two autonomous districts separated by a barren landscape of surface parking and vacant lots.

Tampa's downtown is surrounded by water on three sides, the Hillsborough River on the west, the Garrison Channel on the south, and the Ybor Channel on the east. These waters all flow into Tampa Bay, which is Florida's largest open-water estuary. This unique urban condition has the potential to rejuvenate the city.

Flowscape imagines the transformation of downtown Tampa through the introduction of water into its parched urban core. Instead of just reaching out into the river with piers and walkways, the river is invited into the city. By excavating a canal underneath the expressway, the mouth of the Hillsborough is connected to Ybor Channel, letting the brackish waters circulate through the city. What was once a district of forgotten spaces is now a lush urban marshland. Secondary canals stretch out into the surrounding downtown districts creating a connective blue network. Tampa's already vibrant boating culture is now integrated into the urban and ecological networks of the city.

PARKING +

The surface parking previously occupying this area is consolidated into high-rise *Parking Plus* towers located at the periphery of the new pedestrian-oriented districts. Residents and visitors park at the edge and walk or take rail to their final destinations.

1. The River is Invited Into the City-A Canal is Cut Under the Crosstown Connecting the Tampa Open Estuary to the Garrison and Ybor Channels, Revitalizing the Lush, Interstitial, Forgotten Space Under the Highway Infrastructure.
2. Landscape as Infrastructure.

1

2

3. New Pedestrian Grid is Overlaid Onto the Shifting Shoals of the Tampa Bayou.
4. Landscape as Infrastructure.

An unexpected mix of programs occupies the parking towers to enrich a building type that is, in many cases, the cause of urban blight.

A GREATER GRID

A new pedestrian grid is overlaid onto the shifting shoals of the Tampa Bayou to allow for the flow of walkers, joggers, and cyclists while water and wildlife pass freely below.

The grid takes several forms depending on local conditions: Over wetlands, it adopts the typology of an elevated boardwalk with utilities imbedded within its hollow section. Upland, the grid takes on a more traditional *green street typology*.

LANDSCAPE AS INFRASTRUCTURE

During hurricane season, the landscape mitigates the effects of storm surge force and flooding with a productive park network and tidal salt marshes.

This continuous layered ecosystem attenuates waves, manages the urban watershed, filters interior surface runoff, enhances biodiversity, and introduces a new system of public green space.

In addition to providing habitat and new park space, the riverine islands treat urban runoff through phytoremediation. They are strategically constructed at the mouths of existing storm water culverts, in order to locally filter out pollutants.

Storm water flow sequence: rooftops and streets > bio-swales > streams and canals > downtown bayou > river/channel > bay > gulf > ocean.

A NEW (OLD) VERNACULAR

Flowscape represents an urbanism that submits to natural rhythms. Wetland neighborhoods rise and fall with the tides on buoyant foundations. Forgotten forms of architecture re-emerge as the city reorients itself towards the water. Amphibious structures step out into the water on stilts like flamingo legs. Stilt houses/offices/garages/malls sit high and dry above the bayou, allowing ecological processes to flow below.

AN OPEN NETWORK

A matrix of marine piles dots the shoreline, providing an open-ended framework for architectural and ecological systems. This is the underlying infrastructure of new amphibious buildings, platforms and pathways.

ROW YOUR BOAT (TO WORK)

Boating is an extremely popular pastime in Tampa Bay. On any given day yachts, sailboats, dinghies, jet skis, kayaks, and racing shells can be seen navigating the waters around the city. Boating activities are brought into downtown with a network of maritime infrastructure. Boating is no longer confined to leisure and commerce, now it is imagined as a viable transportation option for downtown residents and tourists. A daily commute might involve a scenic paddle through mangrove flats, up the Franklin St. canal, past a floating coffee shop, and finally coasting into the office slip. The only honking heard during this rush hour is the call of the Great Blue Heron!

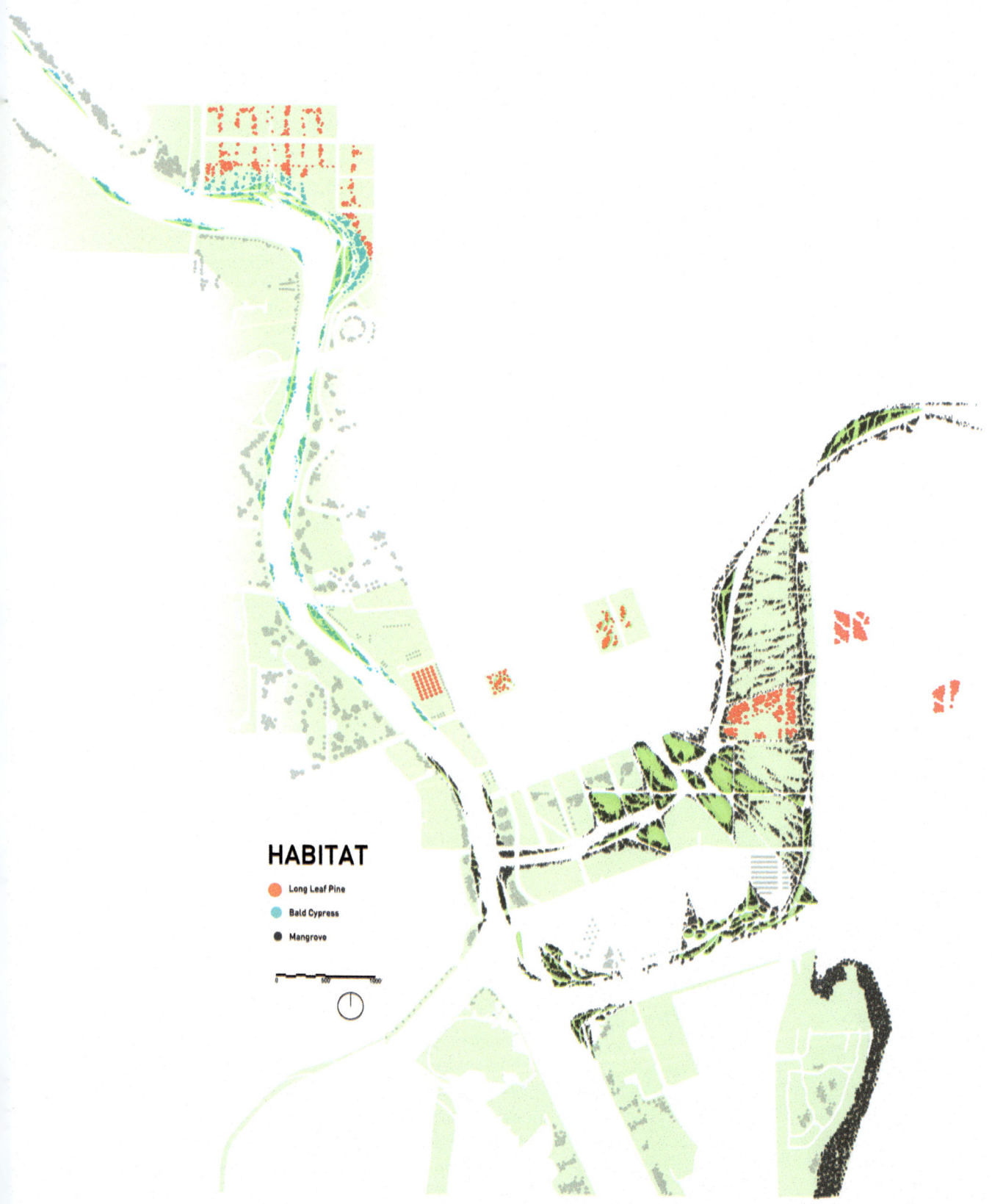

HABITAT

- 🔴 Long Leaf Pine
- 🔵 Bald Cypress
- ⚫ Mangrove

0   500   1000

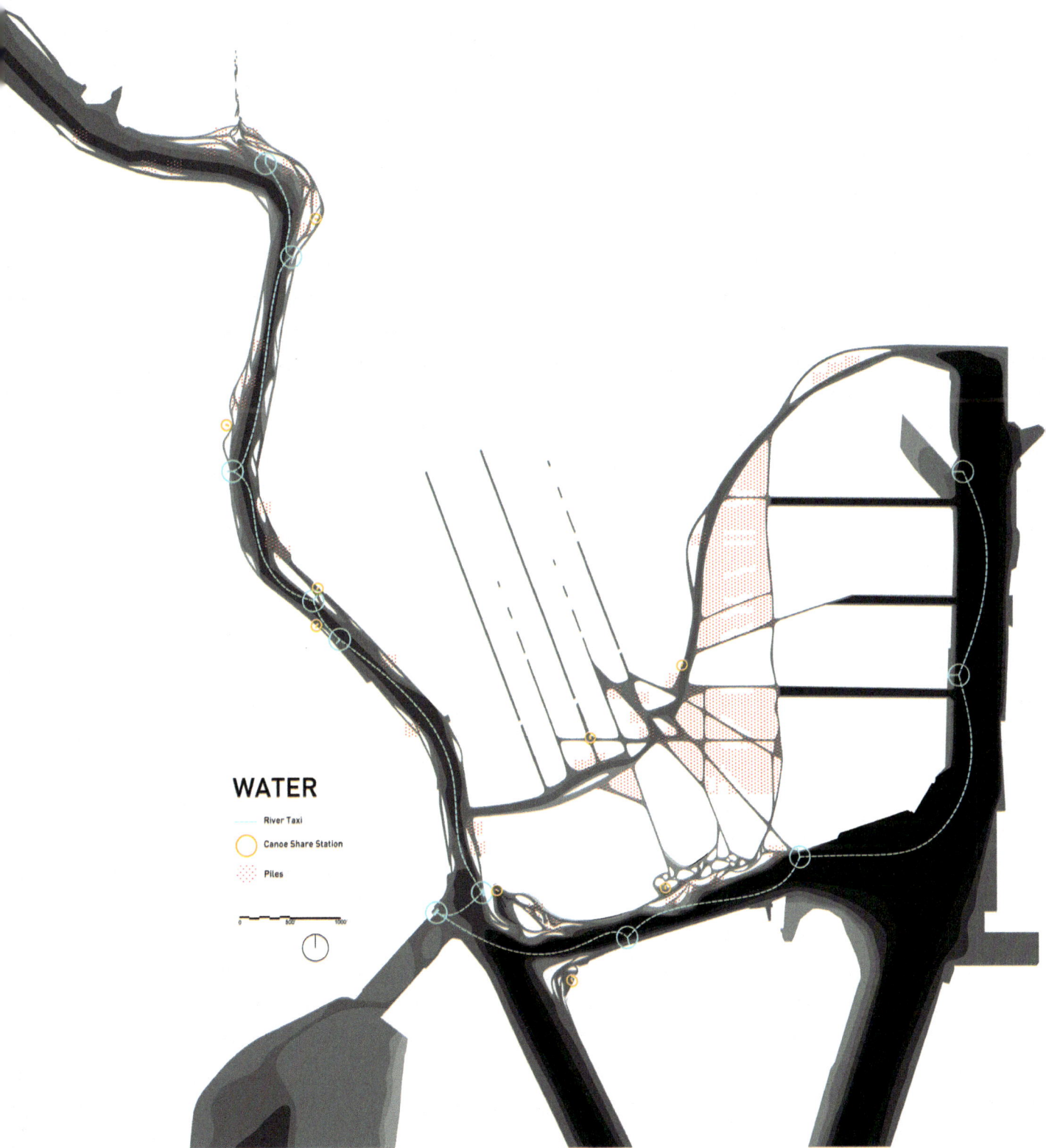

WATER

— River Taxi

◯ Canoe Share Station

⋮⋮⋮ Piles

0   500   1000

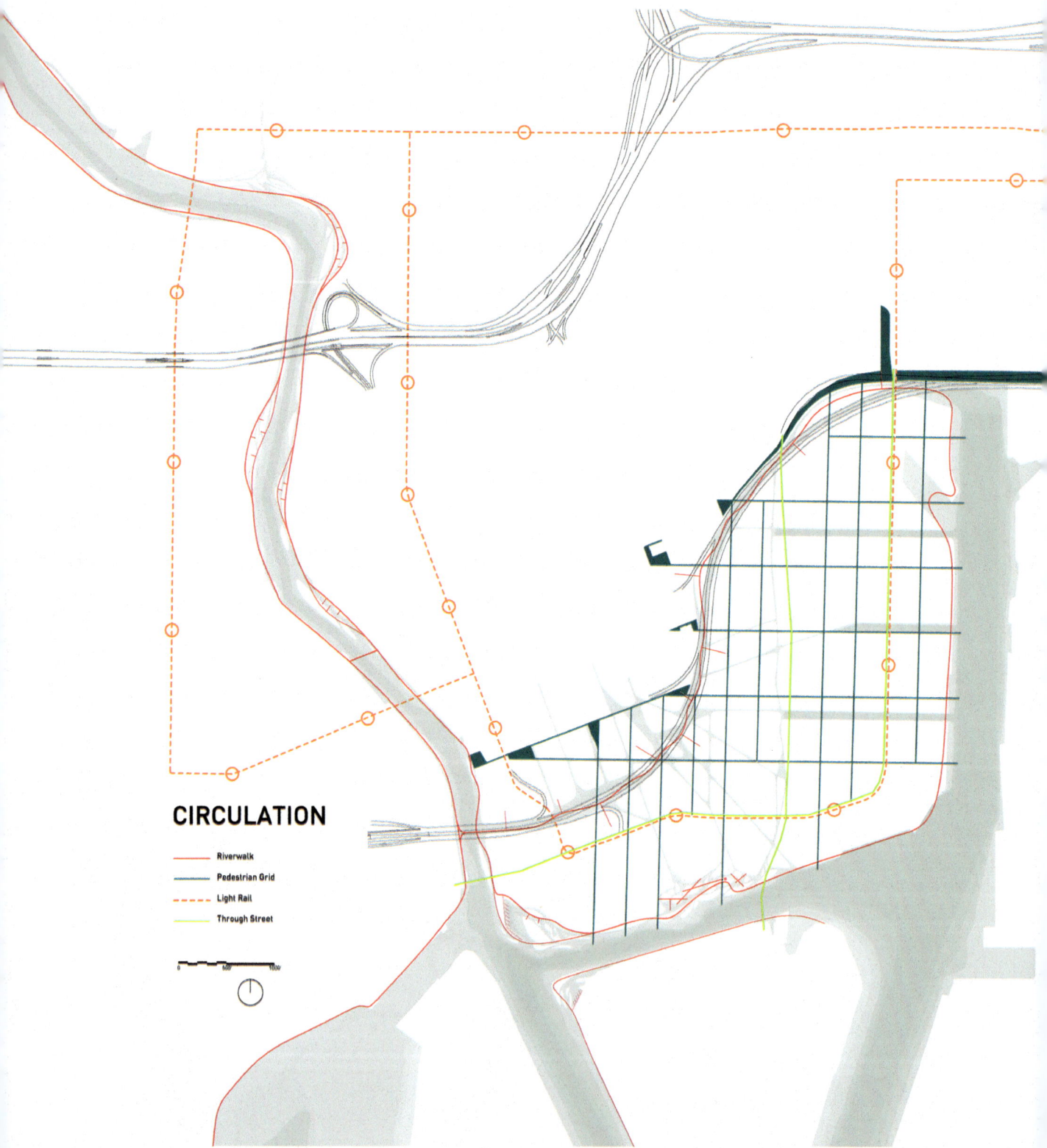

CIRCULATION

——— Riverwalk
——— Pedestrian Grid
- - - Light Rail
——— Through Street

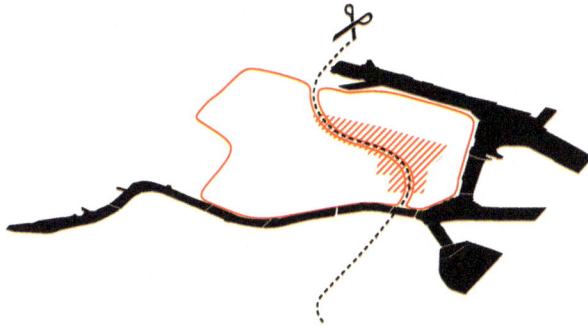

DIVIDE

Downtown bisected by expressway infrastructure

/// 90% Surface parking

◯ Parking district boundaries

----- Expressway

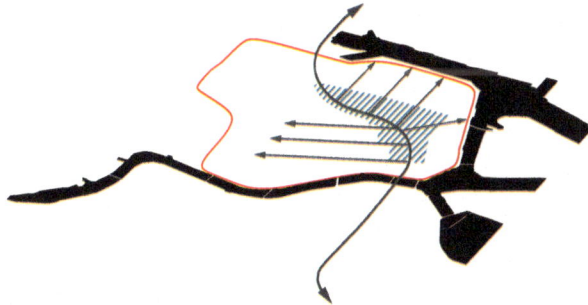

UNITE

Downtown connected by wetland

/// Connective wetland

◯ Connected downtown

↻ New waterways

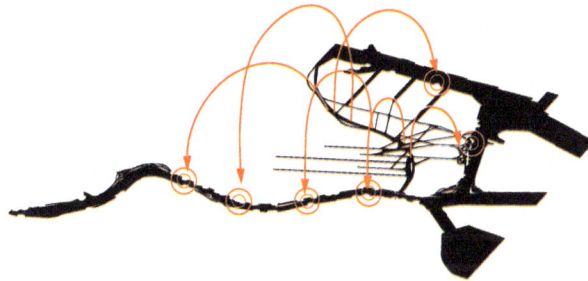

DISTRIBUTE

Riverine islands consructed from excavated material

◉ Stormwater outlets

◯ Movement of rubble / soil from excavation

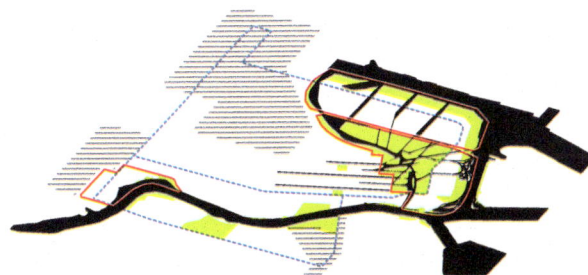

INTEGRATE

Downtown connected by wetland

◯ New downtown districts

≡ Peripheral Neighborhoods

◯ Downtown light rail

▮ Shared open space

[re]Stitch
[re]Silience

Mola + Winkelmueller Architekten GmbH BDA:
A. Mola, L. Mola, P. Adame, M. Prados,
P. Caballero, M. Cabezas, I. Moreno, A. Robotis.

Consultants: Genesis Group,
Lukas Kronawitter, JFS Engineering, WES Berlin,
BWP Berlin, Buro Happold Berlin (first phase).

Berlin, GERMANY + New York, USA + Tampa, USA

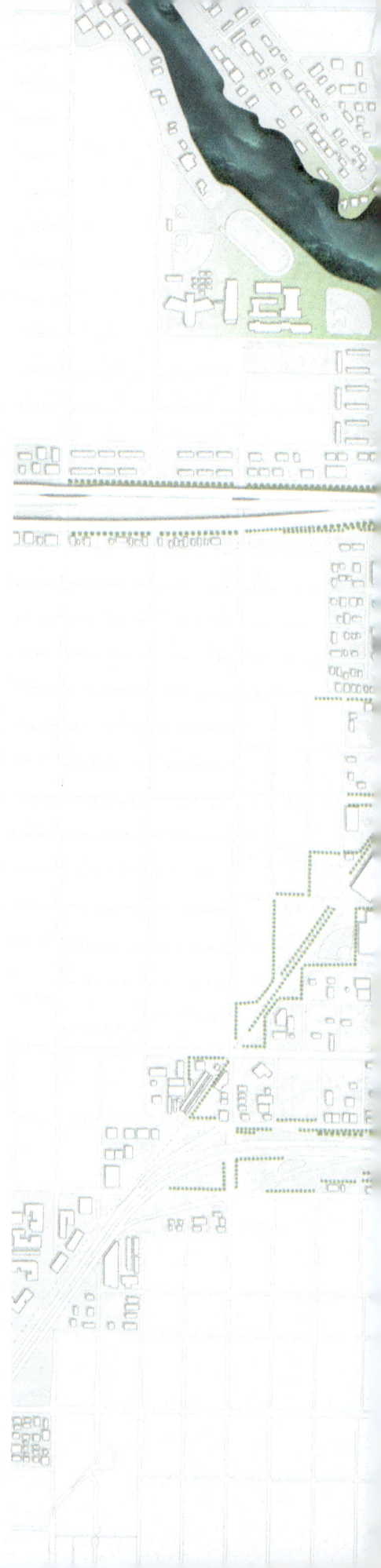

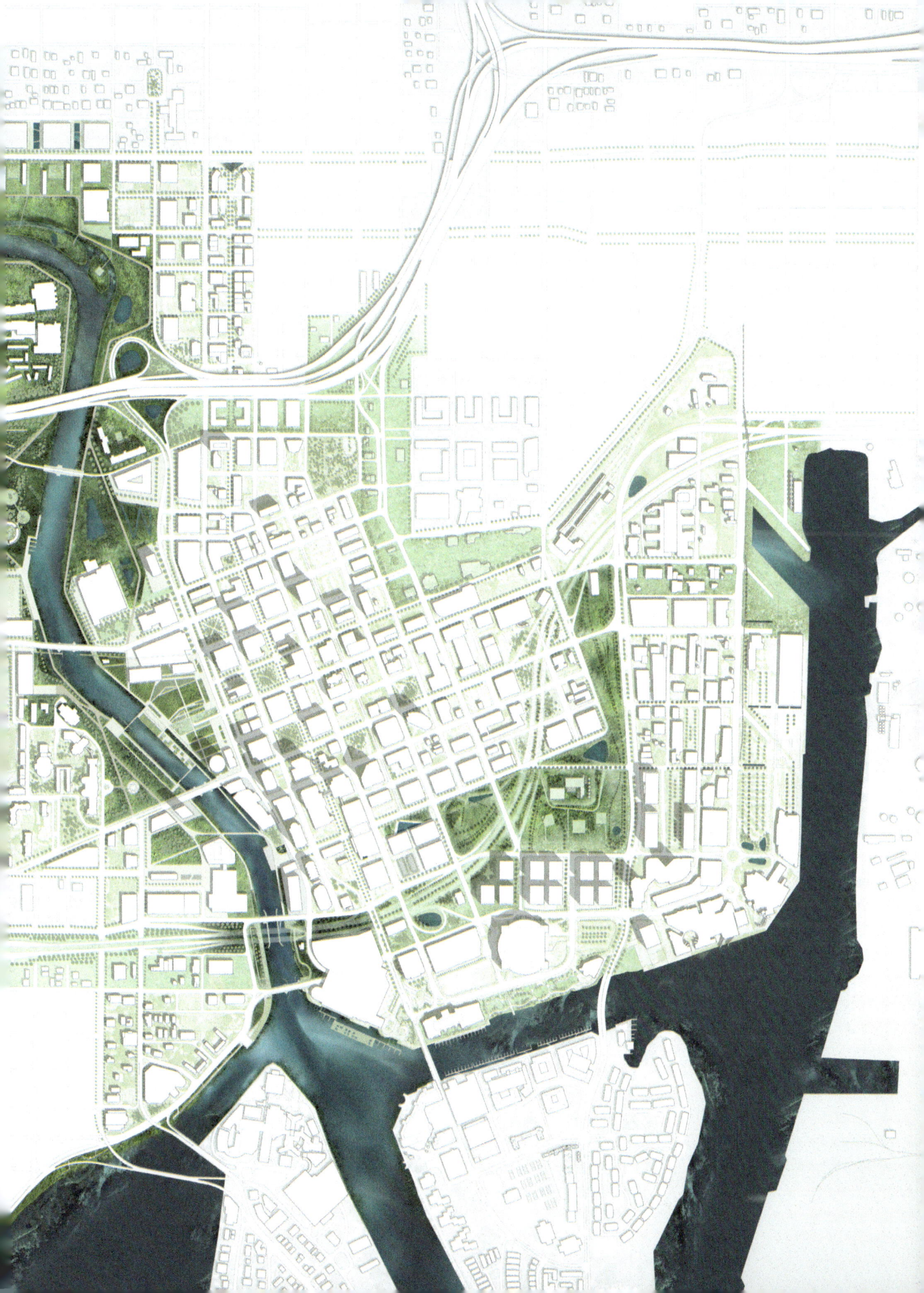

1. Landscape is Transformed into a Malleable Landscape of a Lush, Gridded Archipelago of Urban Islands.
2. Landscape and Ecology Act as Interconnective Corridors Within Tampa's Urban Corridors.
3. Map Illustrates Former Transportation Corridors Which are Transformed into Sustainable Ecological Corridors.

Tampa Bay and the Hillsborough River are critically important ecosystems and vital natural resources that attract and support millions of residents and visitors. However, unsustainable development and lifestyle practices are damaging the local ecosystem, increasing the exposure to storm water flooding, the heat island effect, and water shortages, causing potentially high costs for present and future generations. Additionally, the city of Tampa is increasingly vulnerable to the impacts of climate change. Extreme weather changes resulting in more frequent and intense storms, sea level rise, and higher, bigger, faster storm surges, could cause significant, even catastrophic damage. However, Tampa can transform these environmental challenges into opportunities, by seeking a more ethical and simultaneously mutually beneficial balance between nature and human society.

Our proposed strategy is to transform the landscape into a malleable archipelago of lush, gridded urban islands, joined by landscape corridors, and a functional urban ecosystem designed specifically for the city of Tampa and ecology of the Hillsborough River and Tampa Bay, with the opportunities of each and the limitations of neither. These living urban islands are designed with many functions in mind. Of course they provide valuable and needed public space, but at the same time serve the public through storm water management, potable water use, irrigation, temperature reduction, and air filtration... Sustainable urban storm water drainage systems are integral features throughout the city, managing a large portion of rainwater peaks, saving costs and reducing damage to riparian ecology. These features are specifically engineered into attractive and connective amphibian landscapes. Surface parking lots are turned into Parks-in-lots and overlaid with other uses such as tree nurseries, urban agriculture and community gardens. Buildings will be designed or refurbished to meet sustainable building criteria. A transition from costly space consuming automobile infrastructure to more sustainable forms of transportation such as pedestrian, bike, public transport, E-mobility and car sharing initiatives is also proposed. The dominant one-way street traffic system will be made two-way where possible. A fine grid of land use patterns and variety of parcel sizes will broaden the pool of potential investors, designers and users. The connections across the downtown peninsula will be strengthened through landscaping and destinations. The identity of Franklin Street will be strengthened from its beginning at the YMCA, to its end at the Bay through landscaping, urban furniture and design guidelines. The shading devices, fountains and rain gardens, will serve as unifying elements and Landscape subthemes can provide variety, including community garden restaurants, Teco e-mobility showcase, and pocket parks. The North Franklin Street district can be made more attractive by re-connecting it to the new Hillsborough River

Renaissance Park through slight modifications to the Ashley Street ramp.

The former transportation corridors are converted into an interconnected landscape with sustainable infrastructure. The new Hillsborough River Renaissance Park, Bayshore Rediscovery Park, the Crosstown Park and Channelside Park, each have a particular identity. The new parks will re-stitch the downtown peninsula with the surrounding neighborhoods. The Riverwalk and the new Bayshore Park will become part of a network of tree-lined streets, green corridors and parks. The river and bay edges will be softened and reconnected, giving more space for human and habitat regeneration. The Bayshore seawall is softened, creating a rich ecological park with piers and barrier islands that help protect the neighborhood from storm surge. The Crosstown Park harbors playgrounds, wetland nurseries, solar farms and rain gardens. The railroad corridor is similarly transformed by adding regional passenger rail, cycling, as well as a pedestrian corridor that are combined with urban agriculture and recreation uses.

The new Hillsborough River Renaissance Park is the largest intervention. It reaches and connects the districts. Ecological steps will be taken to repair the river ecological system from its origin to the Bay. Education, water conservation, promoting SUDS (Sustainable Urban Drainage Systems) and the reduction of harmful emissions, are important to restoring the vitality and resilience of this natural resource. The river ecosystem system is given more room and flows uninterrupted through downtown to the bay at the river level. The city fabric stretches above and connects at the bridges. These points are points of density where both systems are connected.

The park celebrates the natural and dynamic relationship between water and coastal wetland, and invites Tampa to explore, play, and learn. The daily tidal rhythms and dry and wet seasons are experienced in the park's rain gardens, pools and fountains. Portions of the Riverwalk float with the tides, while others dive under the bridges, or provide portholes for glimpses into underwater ecosystems and re-naturation measures. The park nurtures the fragile ecosystem and manages rainwater, while also defending the city from water's more destructive tendencies. Park elements and topography are staged for storm surge protection and evacuation for more than a 400-year storm, ensuring that Tampa stays dry and safe.

Urban Development Phases

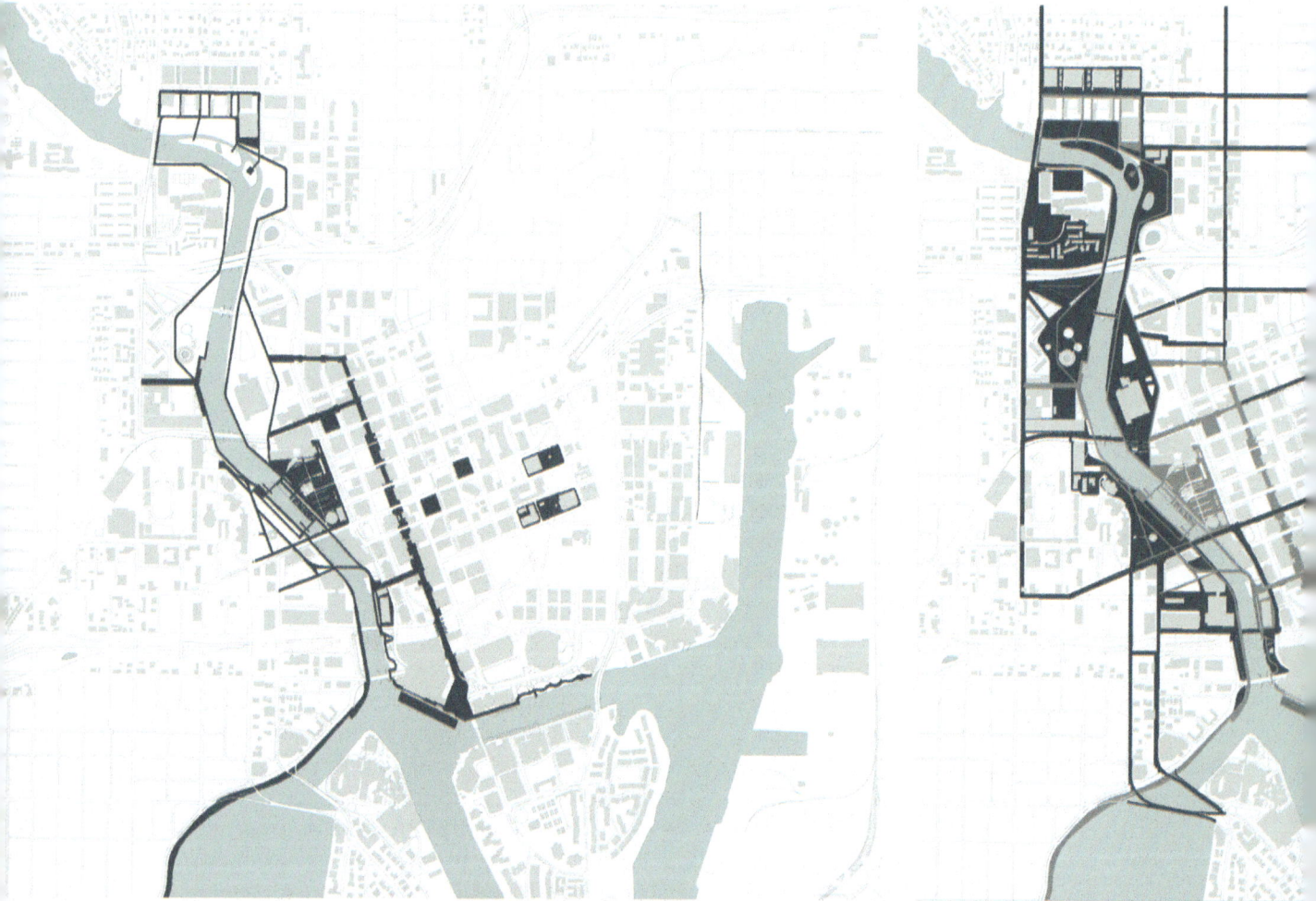

0-5 YEARS

On the water, the central design element in this river park is a modular floating public square bridging the left bank, the University of Tampa, with the Arts District and the CBD. The floating structure is a movable scaffold accommodating numerous programs and ecological infrastructure. It is a storm water storage and purification system that forms part of the water purification strategy where parallel river arms and natural edges are impossible. The locally produced plug-in elements include floating gardens, summer fountains, water instruments, swimming and educational barges.

We hope these measures will help make Tampa a more livable, safe, and resilient place that reconnects its citizens with the beautiful environment that they are privileged to share.

5-15 YEARS

15-20 YEARS

INFRASTRUCTURE DIAGRAM

Legend:
- SHADES
- TIDAL ENERGY
- CRUISE SNIPS / WATER TAXI
- PEDESTRIAN
- SMART GRID
- WATER RECYCLING
- SOLAR PANELS
- WIFI

ECOLOGY DIAGRAM

STITCHES

PERMEABLE AREAS

WETLANDS

SEMIPERMEABLE AREAS

LEVELS

TRAIN

DRAINAGE AREAS

GREEN AREAS

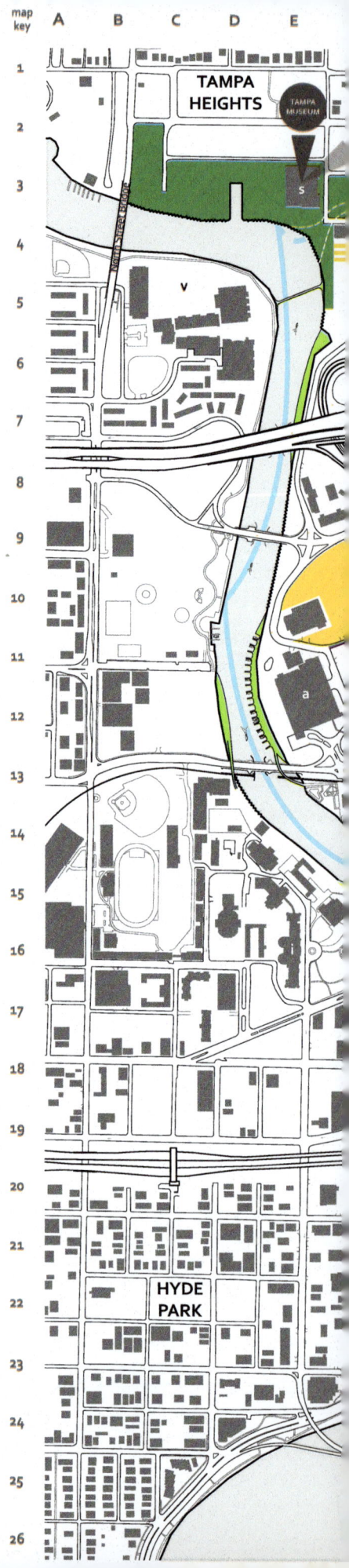

Stitches-Fabrics

Chris Webb and Amarja Chhapwale
Webb-archyrsalis

Mumbai, India

TAMPA
HEIGHTS

TAMPA
MUSEUM

HYDE
PARK

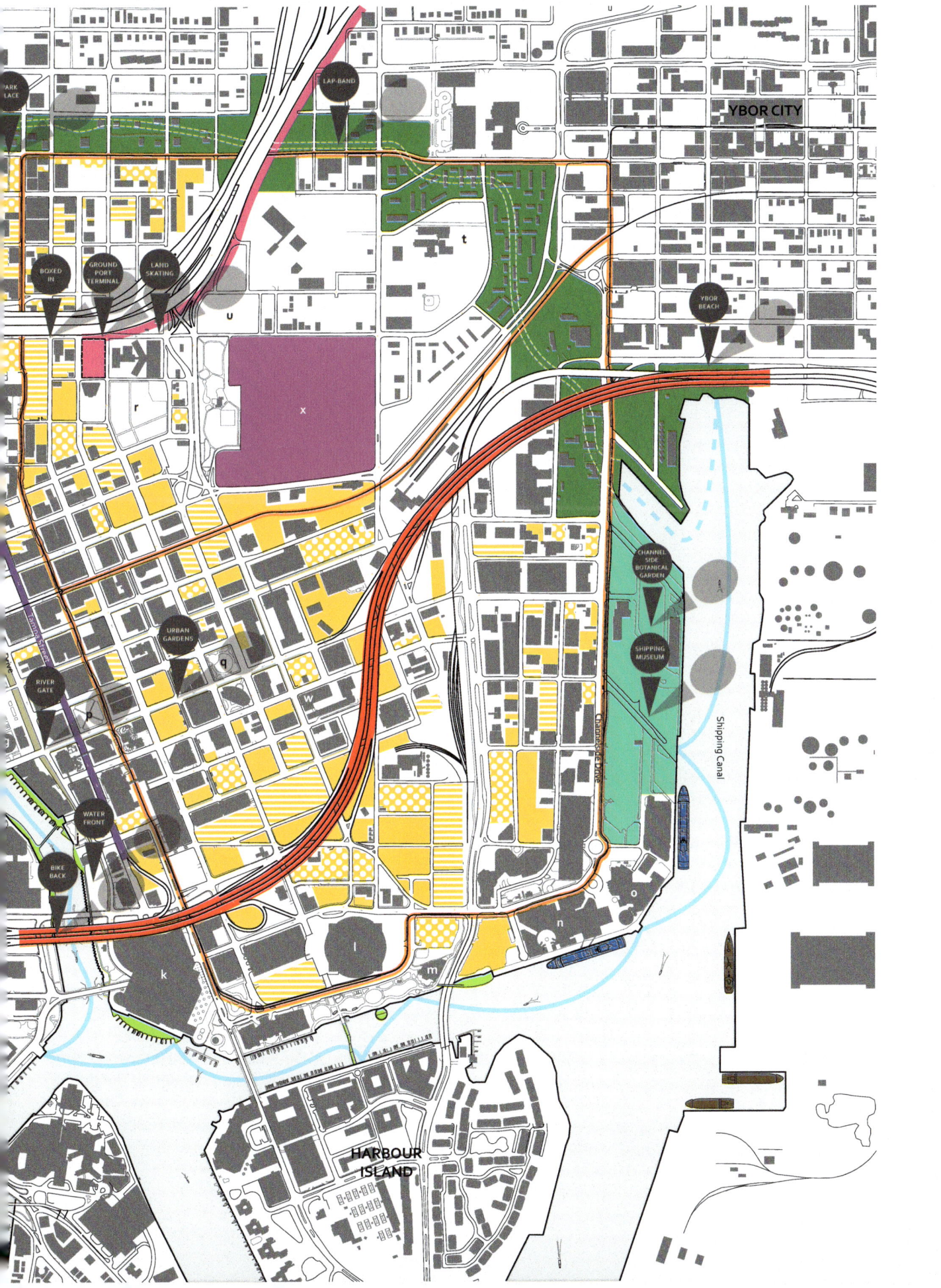

YBOR CITY

PARK
PLACE

LAP-BAND

BOXED
IN

GROUND
PORT
TERMINAL

LAND
SKATING

YBOR
BEACH

t

u

r

x

CHANNEL
SIDE
BOTANICAL
GARDEN

SHIPPING
MUSEUM

Shipping Canal

Channelside Drive

URBAN
GARDENS

q

RIVER
GATE

p

w

WATER
FRONT

o

n

BIKE
BACK

l

k

m

HARBOUR
ISLAND

In a complicated world of uncertainty and tentativeness, urban planners would propose flexible, long-term strategies which anticipate cultural and economic cycles. They would look beyond the borders of their site to recognize the relationship of one parcel to the whole. They would assume that elements of a design may or may not occur, or may only occur in fragments over time. Understanding that many factors would combine in complex ways, they would evaluate and project how a variety of social, technological, economical, ecological, as well as political factors might affect the city. Planners would not focus solely on an isolsated specific area for change, understanding it may have the consequence of simplifying a complex picture, creating distortion or short sightedness. They would not propose transformation at only a specific locality, as it may not be enough to rejuvenate a community. In a world where countries, banks, and corporations are volatile, economies, financing, and sponsorship can change overnight. How, then, would you plan for a shifting landscape?

STITCHES present urban uncertainties. They highlight architectural devices, commerce, or cultural trends, which have a substantial impact on the (re)stitching of Tampa. Each can offer a future towards a more cohesive and ecological Riverwalk and urban core.

Land-Aid: a floating, anchoring, or bridging structure used to bypass areas where current city (infra)structures obstruct the Riverwalk; connecting existing public spaces, and allowing a continuous path from the North Street Bridge to Channelside. Ecological constructions of various compositions, they morph, as needed, through the Riverwalk into low impact bio-filters (mitigating city storm water run-off), shoreline habitats (natural vegetation and sea reefs), and places of public gathering and movement (paths, amphitheatres, restaurants).

Light Rail: an advanced high speed eco-train line, initially connecting Tampa to Orlando, which will become part of an emerging network uniting the urban centres of Florida with major nodes around the US. Providing fast, efficient, and economical travel, the train competes with air and vehicle travel as the primary mode of transportation between urban centres.

Ashley One Way: the transformation of Ashley Street into a one-way, south to north, vehicle route . The existing I275 exit ramp is isolated to Tampa Street providing a primary one-way, north to south, entrance into the city and a dedicated connection to the 618 Crosstown Expressway. Traffic along Ashley Drive is reduced by 50%.

Water Taxi: a local and regional shuttle service around Tampa Bay and the Hillsborough River, which brings people directly to the amenities of the river's edge and adjacencies. This ecological mode of transportation provides direct access between established destination points, while offering new perspectives of the city, as well as introducing new urban typologies and economies.

Big Deal: a new three-tier partnership between the City of Tampa and land owners aimed to reclaim the large number of vacant and car park lots within the urban core (50% of the land). Using revenue bonds to assist in the construction of parking structures; consolidating existing parking lots. Half of the liberated land is allocated to the city for the development of public parks and amenities. The remaining half is allocated for new commercial/residential development facilitated by this new relationship.

8 Train: an extension of Tampa's Streetcar system in and around the city centre using both existing (CSX and StreetCar tracks), as well as new rail lines. The train system encourages Transit Oriented Development and provides Streetcar access within a one half-mile radius to all users within Tampa's city centre.

Sponge Park: a consolidation of the 2,000 surface parking spots located at the Port of Tampa into a multi-level car park to liberate the existing non-porous surface into a natural location for bio-swales and bio-filters to mediate stormwater runoff from the eastern region of the urban core. The remediation softens a visual barrier for Channelside adjacencies, adds security and protection for parked vehicles of port users, and becomes an anchor for the southern end of the Riverwalk.

Bandwidth: aan acquisition of properties between Ybor City and Tampa Heights to develop a green artery directly north of the urban core. The acquirement takes advantage of a sharp financial downturn and stagnant economy, in an area where many of the parcels are undergoing or nearing foreclosure, currently owned by the city/state (right of way land or HUD housing) or vacant. Working in combination with the Hillsborough River and the Channelside shipping canal, the new green belt completes the U-shaped natural boundaries of downtown and (re)defines the urban core of Tampa.

Bikeway: a conversion of the region located beneath the elevated roadway into a green artery for bikers and pedestrians, to (re)join the urban core bifurcated by the 618 Crosstown Expressway. Connecting Hyde Park to Ybor City, the continuous two mile cycling path expands and enhances the trail system of the Riverwalk, and provides green spaces for adjacent communities.

Imports: an all-inclusive in-fill of urban renewal development which supplies residents a blend of commerce and community. Offering playgrounds, theatres, retail shopping, and restaurants, adjacent to apartments and homes, the venture hopes to rejuvenate deteriorating neighbourhoods. The developments expect to enhance established physical and social patterns and set precedence over prior urban renewal strategies.

Cruise Industry: a tourist industry welcoming 900,000 passengers in 2011 (8% increase over 2010), from around the world, which plays a vital role for the local economy. In 2013, the Port will add the NCL Norwegian Star, along with Royal Caribbean's Jewel of the Seas and Carnival's Paradise. Recent events involving the sinking of Costa Concordia off the coast of Italy, Princess Cruise Line's outbreak of the norovirus, and Celebrity's outbreaks of gastrointestinal viruses, have cast a dark cloud over the industry.

Shipping Industry: Florida's largest cargo tonnage port, and one of the nation's largest sea ports. The Port of Tampa, known as an energy gateway, boasts an economic impact of 8$ billion and supports 100,00 jobs. Striking a dichotomy with the current ecological development of the Riverwalk and Hillsborough River, the port looks to protect maritime land and expand marketing and community outreach, while facing the current economic recession. The port is a primary importer of petroleum, coal, and fertilizer, and offers ship boarding and repair.

iCar: a current trend of smaller cars which run on renewable low-cost energy (solar and bio-fuel). This movement reduces the parking footprint and allows passengers closer access to final destinations; altering current parking typologies.

Bio-Lane: the replacement of an existing vehicle lane, in locations of unnecessary road widths and lanes, with natural vegetation and proper drainage, to provide onsite storm water filtration management in the form of bio-swales and bio-filters. The swales filter out harmful pollutants, reduces run-off by 80%, and serves as a precipitation release valve during times of heavy downfall when the river is susceptible to sea level rise.

FABRICS highlight a specific location and project a glimpse into an environment when two or more stitches are crossed and activated. By merging stitches in varying combinations, and coupling these with known facts about the community, variations of plausible futures for the city can be projected. Individually, they narrate the urban condition of a specific location, in their totality they provide an overall narrative for a city looking to become ecological and connective through its (infra)structures.

Ybor Beach: Providing both areas of shade and sun conducive to a wide range of individual and group programmatic activities, the beach becomes Ybor city's social mecca and ecological connector via bicycle, pedestrian, and water taxi to Tampa's Urban core. Natural vegetation and bio-filters provide storm water filtration systems for the local community. In cooperation with the Port of Tampa, as a means to become a catalyst for an emerging eco-Tampa, shipping related programs (primarily ship boarding and repair) are relocated to available parcels along the east bay. Adjacent industrial warehouses are transformed into an emerging arts district.

Lap-Band: Able to acquire a continuous field of land between Ybor City and Tampa Heights, a multi-nodal linear transit corridor develops north of the downtown core. Literally separating the city centre from its suburbs via waterways, downtown Tampa becomes a defined geographical identity within a sprawling polynucleated metropolis. The green artery becomes a backdrop for recreational activities, and mixed-use buildings. The canal extends the Riverwalk around the city, providing a continuous five-mile band for pedestrians, bikers, and boaters, and provides natural vegetation for stormwater mitigation and a flood control channel during times of rapid rainfall.

Tampa Museum: A site dedicated to the arts and culture of the region, provides a bookend to the Riverwalk. Adaptively (re)using the historic Trolley Barn, Tampa's Museum serves both as a gateway to Tampa Heights and a facilitator for environmental awareness and education in the community.

Boxed-In: rReclaiming an inefficient infrastructure, a home for "big box" shopping provides retail outlets sought and preferred by transitioning suburbanites. Interstate adjacencies provide efficient shipping and receiving, and prevents large trucks from entering the urban core. The district becomes a place of destination, and not a place of movement.

Park Place: unable to acquire all parcels to complete a homogenous green artery or during a transition, as land is being acquired, Transit Orientated Developments (TODs) are juxtaposed with pocket parks of various programs to create activity centres north of the Unable to acquire all parcels to complete a homogenous green artery or during a transition, as land is being acquired, Transit Orientated Developments (TODs) are juxtaposed with pocket parks of various programs to create activity centres north of the downtown core. The TODs serve as pedestrian oriented places with mixed-income residential communities linked to the downtown core via the Tampa Streetcar.

Bike Back: Linking downtown Tampa to Hyde Park via a dedicated bridge provides connectivity and extends bicycle/pedestrian travel to Ybor City. The bridge provides a protected calm refuge for new perspectives and recreation within the city.

Channelside Botanical Garden: The effects of a retracting cruise and shipping industry, support the creation of a local and regional tourist destination. A bookend to the Riverwalk, the garden completes an expansive three mile U-shaped pedestrian/bicycle path around Tampa. The garden becomes a local amenity, an anchor for the community, and redefines the eastern side of the city as a tourist destination, rather than as an outlying community of the downtown core.

Rivergate: The gateway from Tampa's core to the Hillsborough River, the Riverwalk is widened and extended, softening the existing fractured edge of the

downtown core with amenities along the waterway. The reclaimed north-south vehicular four lane is (retro) fitted with natural vegetation (bio-swales) and becomes the linear filter for the western side of the city.

Waterfront: The Hillsborough River shoreline is continuously connected from the North Street Bridge, to the north, to Channelside, in the southeast. Providing direct crosslinks to major surrounding nodes (U. of Tampa, Hyde Park, Harbour Island) the river's edge becomes the ecological and infrastructural network of the city. With both soft and hard edge surfaces, the shoreline hosts a wide range of activities, wild life, and vegetation. Existing structures adjacent to the Riverwalk (re)program to offer coffee shops, restaurants, and bars facing the river, and the Hillsborough River becomes the day and nightlife hub for the city.

Urban Gardens: An increase of public parks and trending away from automobiles as its primary means of

transportation, downtown Tampa's identity as a "alpha car city" is replaced by a "city of gardens." The pedestrian friendly urban core attracts businesses looking to relocate, and offers amenities to attract commuters back downtown on the weekend. The porous urban core mitigates stormwater run-off during times of high precipitation, and introduces natural vegetation and wildlife into a once impermeable environment.

Groundport Terminal: At the intersection of high-speed rail, Streetcar, automobile, bus, and pedestrian/bicycle interchange, this once "non-place" becomes a gateway to Tampa and Tampa's gateway out of town. The once exclusively car-parked underbelly of I275 is (re)programmed with commercial shops catering to the needs of the traveller. Tampa is externally and internally connected, reducing a burdened roadway system, once heavily dependent on the lone occupant.

Shipping Museum: With a trade industry looking to advocate its relationship to the region, the Port of Tampa opens a maritime museum whose role is to preserve and illustrate the history of its industry. Building upon environmental awareness and education, and adding to the established row of museums along the waterfront, the facility bookends the Riverwalk and offers a public space of natural vegetation to the neighbouring Channelside community.

Landskating: Countering the (pre)programmed emotion of master planned communities, residual spaces of the city become playgrounds for Tampa's youth. These social attractors provide opportunities for economic growth in previously redundant spaces, as well as amenities of attraction for undecided parents looking to relocate within the urban core.

Honorable Mentions

Pleating Tampa

Pleat, Re-pleat, Repeat

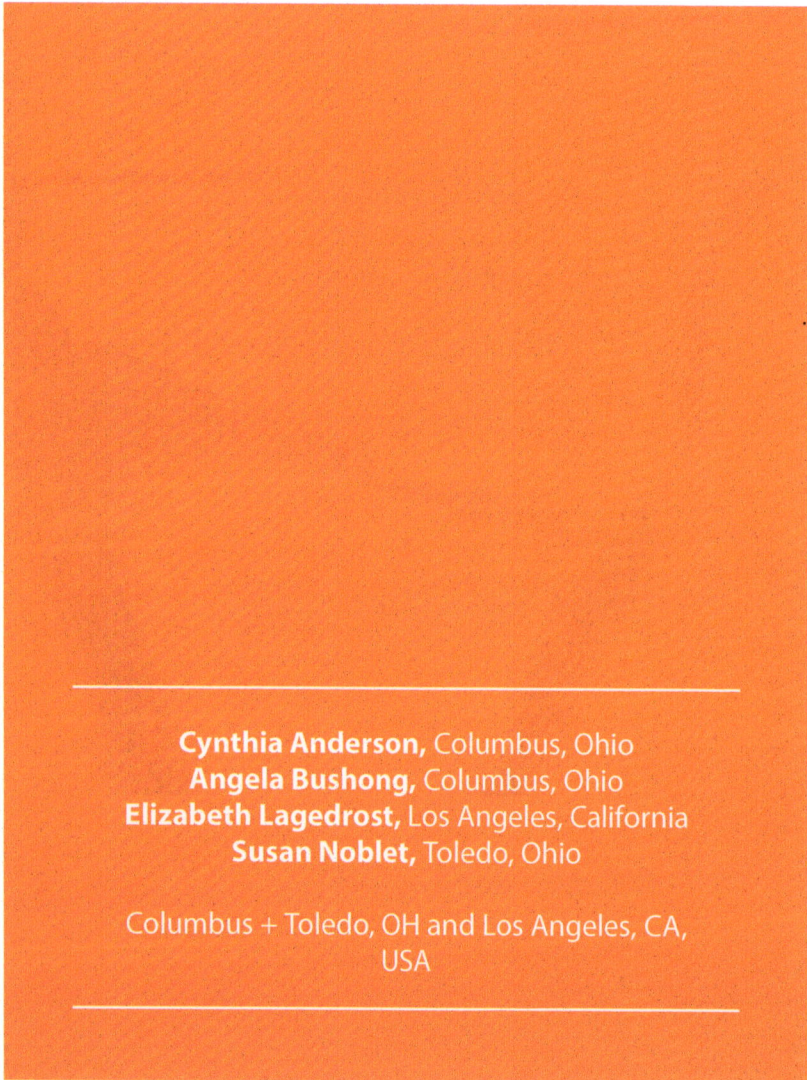

Cynthia Anderson, Columbus, Ohio
Angela Bushong, Columbus, Ohio
Elizabeth Lagedrost, Los Angeles, California
Susan Noblet, Toledo, Ohio

Columbus + Toledo, OH and Los Angeles, CA,
USA

CONNECTIVITY

BUS

BIKE

TROLLEY

TRAIN

INFRASTRUCTURE

STORMWATER MITIGATION

GREEN ROOF

BEACH

SOLAR PANELS

ECOLOGIES

PARKLAND

GREEN PATHWAYS

PRODUCTIVE LAND

HABITAT

PLACES

MUSEUM

RESIDENTIAL

EDUCATIONAL

GARAGE

OH-LA COLLABORATIVE

OH-LA Collaborative is a team of four former Ohio State University class-mates in the graduate Landscape Architecture program. We are fairly recent graduates and have enjoyed continuing our studio collaboration, although now that we are across the country, we do so virtually. Our varied experiences and talents allow us to develop interesting imaginative design concepts to address challenges of livability and sustainability in today's urban setting. Layering ecological, social and economic functions and considering existing urban infrastructure is our prime objective and approach to our concepts.

PLEAT:
a type of fold formed by doubling fabric back upon itself and securing it in place, making a wide piece of fabric narrower; used to shape or allow for freedom of movement.

Pleating Tampa will create a city of vibrant, multilayered activity, built upon the downtown's existing strengths and infrastructure. The proposed strategies also work to reshape Tampa as a leader in sustainable energy generation and urban ecological management. Four areas serve as focal pleats for new development and the layering of activity, action, energy and ecology: the crosstown activity pleat, a new museum district, the river edge eco-park and the performative storm water area to the northwest. These areas are connected to each other and to existing features of Tampa's downtown through a series of pleated pedestrian pathways, bus and rail-based rapid transit, a central park core and retail axes. The approaches proposed aim to "pleat Tampa" to reshape the city by the intensifying of program and re-envisioning infrastructure and working ecologies.

The existing elevated Crosstown Expressway infrastructure defines a strong multilayered pleat

through downtown, which features a bicycle path at grade and a series of programmatic interventions. The 'activity pleat' includes an outdoor concert area, food truck court, Skate Park, and connections to the southern transit exchange. The transitions between zones are denoted by public art installations that are read at a series of speeds and elevations, from the highway above, to cyclists and pedestrians at grade. A new layer of this crosstown pleat takes shape above the highway with net supporting solar panels that generate energy for the activity below, and the needs of new residential and cultural development nearby.

Between the crosstown activity pleat and the Florida Aquarium, a science and technology museum is the central element of a proposed development that includes a new transit facility. An integral part of the museum campus, is a storm and gray water filtration area. The system features phytoremediation as the means of cleansing wastewater by capturing output from the existing storm sewer infrastructure and surrounding buildings, directing the water through a

series of filtration pleats. The educational emphasis of the museum is carried into the filtration pleats through signage and docents describing the ecological systems and principles at work, as well as the benefits of limiting storm water runoff into the river. The cleansed water output will be directed to new industry located both to the north, as well as to the east of the museum campus, creating the basis for a closed-loop industrial system to emerge in the Channelside area.

Tampa's ecological and cultural connection to the river is emphasized by a long, folding and unfolding pleat of eco-park along the river edge. The pleat fans at the convention center, providing a set of formal spaces for gathering, interspersed with vegetated habitats for local ecologies. Traveling north along the river, a bicycle and pedestrian path skirts a softened rivers edge, connecting the Kiley Gardens, Curtis Hixon Park and the Tampa Museum of Art (TMA) campus to riverine ecologies. Beyond the museum, the pleat refolds and terminates in the northwest performative storm water area- focused on managing runoff from surrounding buildings and highway, providing recreational area in spaces that were once asphalt lots.

PLEATING

The proposed design approach, by pleating Tampa, aims to increase the density of connection, function and activity throughout the core. "Pleats" layer two functions; "repleats" contain at least three-layered programs. Green roofs cap garages and new development; new river habitats layer with storm water management and social gathering spots. To the southeast, layering education, art, water, cultural center and entertainment, create a vibrant "repleat" that appeals to Tampa residents and visitors alike.

CONNECTIVE PLEATS

The pleating strategy features the addition of pedestrian pleats through the core of Tampa, and along both sides of the river. The pedestrian pleats replace lanes along Ashley and Twiggs and complement the existing rapid transit corridor and layer vegetation, human activity and storm water mitigation. Additional rapid bus transit loops and bicycle routes enhance the ability

for residents to travel to the edge of central Tampa by auto or train and shift to bike or bus to complete their commute. Bicycle routes also connect to Ybor City. Commuter rail is extended across the northern edge and along the eastern edge of the city. Transit hubs provide means to transfer among modes of travel.

ECO-PLEATS

Habitats are re-introduced, the urban heat island effect is limited, and storm water is managed through the ecological pleating of Tampa's fabric. The river edge is pleated with a series of structures that soften the river edge, house a pedestrian walkway, and introduce habitat for aquatic animals and vegetation. To the north, two large multi-functional eco-areas provide storm water filtration; one also serves as an urban tree nursery. "Pedestrian pleats" layer a pedestrian thoroughfare and an attractively vegetated storm water swale, introducing ecological connections through central Tampa. At the new science museum campus to the southeast, the ecological pleat area emphasizes

Stormwater Pleats Diagram

Pleating Diagram

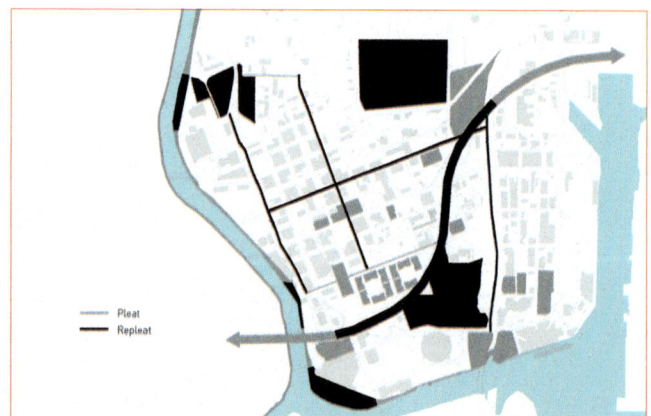

education, storm water management, and social gathering for the Forum and museum. The pedestrian/infrastructure pleat features a net structure that rises over the crosstown highway and serves as a skeleton for cooling, shading, climbing vegetation and for energy generation through a solar array. Green roofs top all new development and are retrofit on existing garages.

STORMWATER PLEATS

Proposed eco-pleats throughout the city mitigate the effect of heavy rains and runoff. In the core of Tampa, the large infiltration areas capture runoff from the existing storm infrastructure. Water discharge into the river is minimized by increased infiltration within the city; the ecological areas running along the river edges also slow the velocity of remaining discharge in order to create more stable aquatic habitats. The infiltration zone at the science museum campus has an additional function of cleansing grey water produced on the site; this cleansed water will ultimately serve as an input for closed-loop industrial development that will emerge in later phases.

PLEATED PHASING

The pleating strategy unfolds across three phases. During Phase I, the eco-pleats and the cultural areas are developed to ameliorate storm runoff and create an in-town attraction for visitors and residents. The Crosstown Expressway activity pleat begins to connect the southeast with central Tampa; the Hillsborough River eco-pleats begin to soften the river edge and introduce new habitat. Rapid bus transit, bicycle ways and a system of transit hubs speed movement through the city and establish the structure for removing sur¬face parking in Phase II. The emphasis in Phase II is to provide an opportunity for infill development on previously vacant or surface parking lot. New consolidation garages are constructed along the rapid transit lines. All new development is designed in order to limit the impact on the environment: mixed use, with on-site water filtration, green roofs and alternate energy generation. Structures will have zero set back. Phase III projects introduce a closed-loop industrial sector at central Channelside and additional mixed-use development.

Connective Pleats Diagram

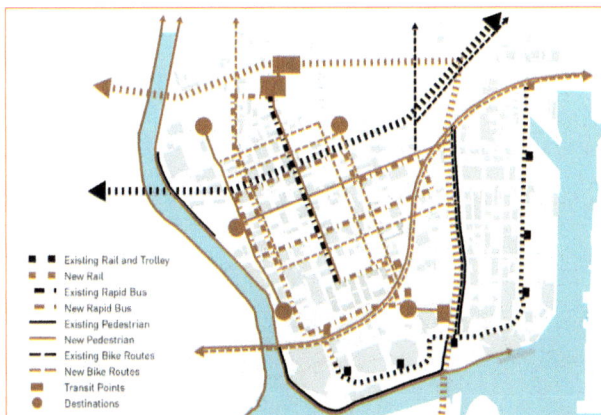

Eco-Pleats Diagram

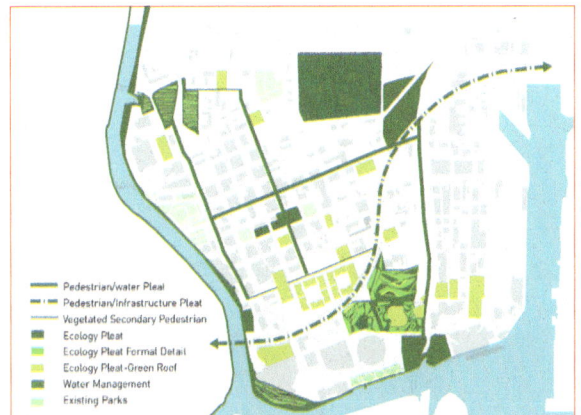

Rehydrate Tampa

Bryan Hanes-Studio Bryan Haynes

Philadelphia, PA

REHYDRATE TAMPA

A new water cleansing, infiltration and recycling infrastructure will become the armature for neighborhood redevelopment throughout downtown Tampa. Currently, bulkheads and dams drain the landscape, divorcing the city from the hydrologic cycle. The infrastructural framework will bring the city back into intimate contact with our need for, and impact on the water that surrounds us.

Employing a network of grey water recycling systems, hydroponic green walls, algae farms, vegetated canals, and large-scale wetlands, the city of Tampa will reuse 100% of its wastewater and graywater, and cleanse storm water before returning it to the Hillsborough River. By restoring freshwater flows to the River, the system will re-establish the salinity gradient needed to sustain estuarine ecosystems in the Hillsborough and Tampa Bays. It will also mitigate potable water demands on the River and aquifer. Finally, this water infrastructure will become the framework for new industry, housing and neighborhood typologies to emerge in the core of the city.

POLLUTION SOURCES

The once pristine Hillsborough River has borne the brunt of regional development, coming under increasing attack from pollution. The rural northern and central portions of the watershed primarily consist of rangeland, pasture, and agriculture, including citrus groves and row crops. Nutrient-enriched effluent from agricultural and urban storm water runoff, and industrial wastewater generated by food processing, fertilizer and insecticide facilities continually, contaminate the River and Bay. Consequently, the two main problems facing the Hillsborough are excess nitrogen and deficient oxygen. Nitrogen loading in the bay has significantly reduced vital sea grass beds – an indicator of bay health. The excess nutrients fuel algae blooms that cut off sunlight and deplete oxygen levels, creating "dead zones" in the bay where fish, mollusks, and crustaceans cannot survive.

THE THIRSTY RIVER

The Hillsborough River is thirsty. Once a source of abundant freshwater flowing into Tampa Bay, the Hillsborough is now heavily relied upon to supply an increasingly large portion of Tampa's potable water supply, leaving the River dry and salty as it approaches the bay. The bay depends on a steady freshwater diet, in order to create the highly fertile nursery areas and low-salinity habitats, those that the estuary's ecosystems and celebrated sport fisheries require. Low-salinity tidal marsh is an important and rare habitat for juvenile fish spawning and countless wading birds. Restoring freshwater flows to the lower Hillsborough and to Tampa Bay are critical to long-term ecological viability.

INSATIABLE DEMAND

Demand for freshwater in Florida has increased dramatically in the rapidly growing region. Heavy burdens on ground and surface waters has resulted in shrinking lakes, vanishing wetlands, dried up wells and a surplus of sinkholes. As the Tampa region grows, so does its need for freshwater, which will put increasing ecological stress on the aquifer, the rivers and bays.

NEW PLUMBING

Two interlaced systems of water flow define the neighborhood districts of downtown Tampa. The Vena Cava, or main return arterial of floodwater and storm surge into the city, directs water either into large-scale wetlands or the algae gardens. As the water passes through these systems, it either infiltrates the aquifer, or flows back into the capillary system. The capillary network is a series of fine-grained vegetated canals that define the social spaces and pedestrian-friendly thoroughfares of Tampa Heights, the Waterworks District, and portions of the Central Business District.

TAMPA HEIGHTS

Tampa Heights is finely threaded with the capillary system. The gray water generated from each single-family house is partially filtered through an underground filtration tank system, before being released to the vegetated canals that weave through each block. These canals start off rather narrow at the city's interior, and slowly widen to accommodate increased flows at they reach the river. The canal network provides a new set of pedestrian pathways that encourage a variety of recreational uses and opportunities for socializing.

FRESHWATER AS LIFEBLOOD

Challenging conventional notions of the front and back yard, the spaces in the front maintain street activity, while the back is canal-focused. Gray water is collected from adjacent homes, taken through a series of underground filtration tanks, and is then released into the path-lined channels of water and vegetation. The water infrastructure thus serves as an orienting device for the community while the filtration process becomes a continuous visual event that links and activates spaces between neighbors and homes.

THE WET POCKETS

Three large-scale wetlands interrupt Tampa's city grid, creating urban parks with a highly programmed ecological

mandate. Each of the three are connected to the Grand Canal in order to receive flood surges, storm water overflows, and treated wastewater from the algae farms. They are also connected to the capillary system, both receiving as well as releasing water depending on the pressure gradient.

THE ALGAE GARDENS

Several vacant lots adjacent to the Grand Canal host algae farms that feed off of the nutrient-laden storm water and Hillsborough Bay overflows. These farms create a micro-industry for the city; a related research center affiliated with the University of Tampa is established. The algae gardens separate different strains of algae into growing cells, creating a surreal and multicolored landscape.

THE CAPILLARIES

Tampa's street grid is colonized by a network of vegetated canals that allow storm water and floodwaters to be cleaned and redistributed throughout the city before slowly flowing back to the river. These canals reconfigure the widest east-west avenues in Tampa's central business and government districts, cutting back the number of traffic lanes, and introducing pedestrian-friendly and shaded promenades. In Tampa Heights and the Waterworks District, these watery threads connect both to townhouse, as well as to detached housing graywater recycling tanks. Water that is not reused is released to the system, is allowed to flow back towards the river. During storm events, these channels can flow inland towards one of three large-scale wetlands, creating a network of floodwater release valves.

THE LIVING WALLS

In both the Central Business and Channelside Districts, high and mid-rise mixed-use development replaces open lots and excess surface parking. These buildings incorporate hydroponic vertical green walls on their facades that function both as graywater recycling systems for the building. Each residential and commercial tenant is connected to the system, which holds and filters gray water for either reuse or discharge into civic-scaled water features.

THE VENA CAVA

The Grand Canal is highly managed in order to maximize the filtration of incoming water from the Hillsborough Bay during storm surges and in anticipation of sea level rise. The Grand Canal will channel flows back into the city, where it will be captured for industrial use in several adjacent algae bio-fuel facilities. The excess nitrogen will be extracted through the production process, before the water is released to one of three major wetland pods along its spine. Huge bio-filtration reservoirs, these wetlands will clean the largely brackish, nutrient-laden water, before releasing it back into the aquifer or to the canal system that laces the city.

Waterworks District

Hinging off the water infrastructure of the city, the Townhouse District orients homes to block interiors featuring views to a string of vegetated canals. Townhouses of three to four stories create a level of neighborhood density, while distinguishing it from the nearby downtown fabric.

The Channelside District

Mid-rise, mixed-use buildings and courtyard civic spaces recolonize the Channelside District, attracting a new population of downtown residents. The buildings house retail on the ground floor to enliven the streetscape, while parking is concealed on the second and third floors. Residential units float above, and overlook civic-scaled water collection and piazza-like courtyards down below. The facades of the buildings are cladded with hydroponic green walls that filter 100% of the gray water production in the building. This water is partially recycled into flush toilets, and the remaining is passed through a 2nd-tier filtration system before being released to the central plaza's water features.

Re-stitch Tampa the Sub-urban Mix

3/4 mile to the city
5 min on bicycle

ban space
le hub

3/4 mile to the city
5 min on bicycle

New chan

arki_lab+ Jeanette Frisk and Rasmus Frisk

Copenhagen, Denmark

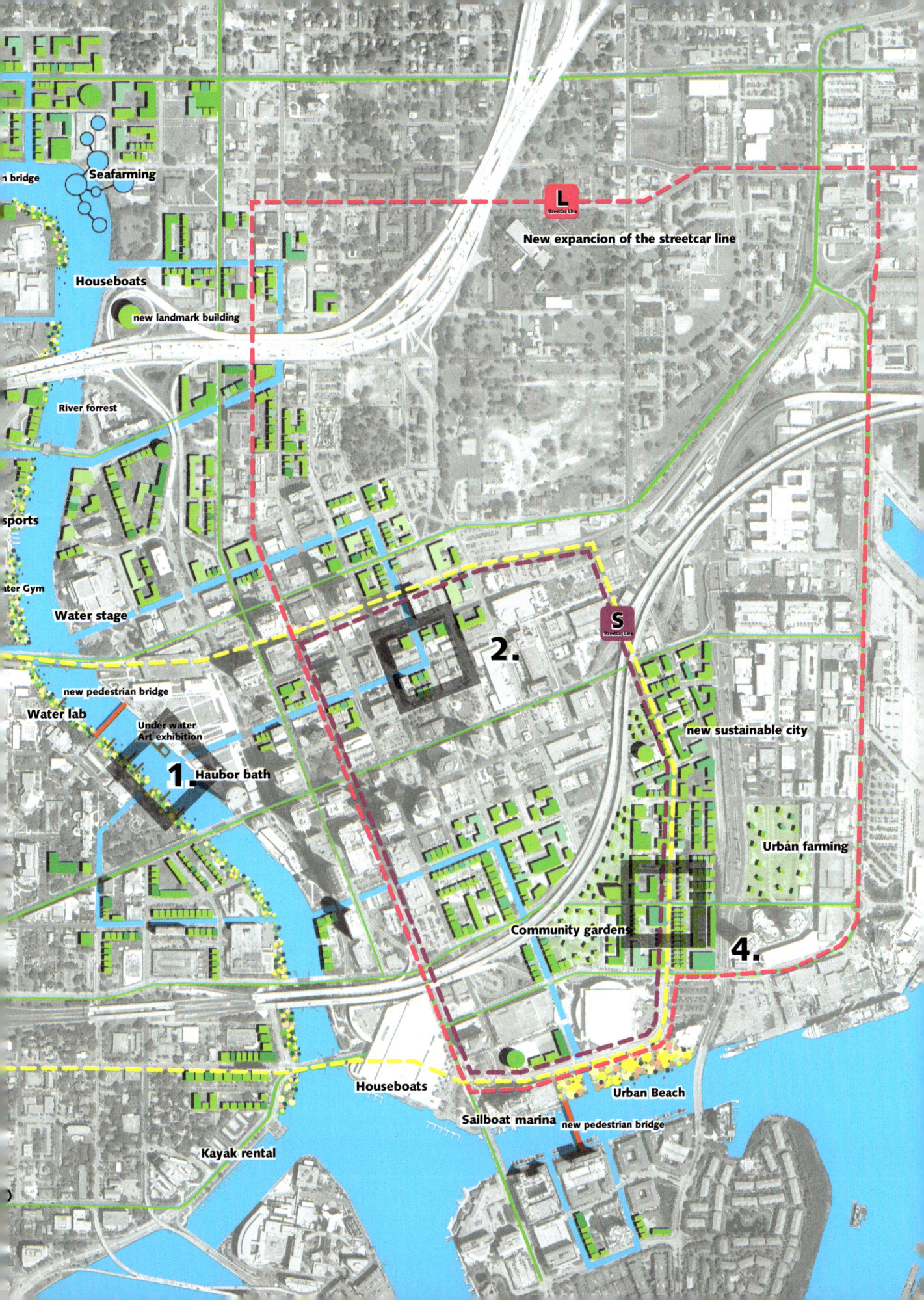

Seafarming

n bridge

Houseboats

new landmark building

New expancion of the streetcar line

L StreetCar Line

River forrest

sports

ter Gym

Water stage

2.

S StreetCar Line

new pedestrian bridge

Water lab

Under water Art exhibition

new sustainable city

1. **Haubor bath**

Urban farming

Community gardens

4.

Houseboats

Urban Beach

Sailboat marina

new pedestrian bridge

Kayak rental

1. MOVE THE CITY CENTER TO THE RIVER

Move the downtown center as it exists currently, and make the river both a new spine, as well as the new center of the city. Install a public and continuous promenade stretching along the entire waterfront in order to connect different waterfront areas and to ensure that all people have access to the water.

2. WORK AND LIVE IN THE CITY

Cities for people = Sustainable Cities

There have to be people living in the city in order to avoid dead and abandoned city centers after 5 pm. The reduction of CO_2 by locating workplaces close to Residential areas is 10 times more effective than simply insulating new buildings from the normal standard to a higher level.

3. ACTIVATE THE RIVER

Develop the waterfront into a city destination.

Celebrate the waterfront and develop it into a fabulous place for people through public spaces of excellent quality and public functions in adjacent buildings.

4. STITCHING THE CITY TOGETHER

The river currently exists as a barrier within the city. In order to better connect Tampa, we need to think reconceptualize its infrastructure, thus making crossing the river more straightforward. Residential and commercial areas should be better distributed on both sides of the river, in order to create a lively and safe urban environment.

5. BRINGING THE WATER TO THE CITY

Introducing new canals into the city grid is the best method for storm water flood management. It also helps to slow down traffic, and to create a completely different set of urban spaces within the city. It also creates and new way of moving in and around the city using the water.

6. DENSITY + DIVERSITY = PROXIMITY

Develop the empty lots and parking areas into new buildings with a good mixed use and functional flexibility. Create new alternative parking lot options that do not occupy the ground floor level. All new developments should have a green roof in order to help absorb rainwater and lower urban air temperatures.

7. MAKE GOOD PUBLIC TRANSPORT

There need to be better alternatives to using your car in the city, alternatives that are easy, convenient and less polluting. Expand the existing streetcar network by introducing 3 new loops connecting downtown, the university grounds and suburbs.

8. MAKE RECREATIONAL LINKS TO THE CITY

Develop new green recreational routes to and from the city. Allow people the option of choosing a different, healthier and non-polluting way of getting to and from work.

Encourage people to bike, by establishing new bicycle hubs in the suburbs by introducing a new Tampa city bike arrangement that is convenient and available for all.

9. INCREASE WALK-ABILITY AND BIKE-ABILITY

Ensure that the development of a clear way-finding system is developed. Additionally, encourage people to walk or bike instead as opposed to driving causing them to be stuck in traffic where they loose precious time by having to find parking. This is accomplished by putting another easier, faster, and more convenient as well as safer option on people's mental map.

10. DEVELOP A NETWORK OF PUBLIC SPACES AND DESTINATIONS

Connect the public spaces and city destinations with pedestrian-friendly routes in order to create attractive and varied sequences of spaces within the city.

11. CREATE A HIERARCHY OF STREETS AND SPACES

Create streets and spaces of different importance, use, size and character; city, neighborhood, and local spaces to provide a varied and legible network.

12. OUR (RE)-STITCHED TAMPA

Tampa is an Ecological city, with a better human-scale Infrastructure, well connected and legible in its context - with an emphasis on putting people first in planning.

13. HARDWARE BEFORE SOFTWARE

We need to change the mind-set of traditional urban planning practices. Instead of doing buildings first, and hoping for a life to emerge after, we need to flip that thought. We need to first provide Life, by activating the existing Riverfront (phase 1), and by then providing a new space by introducing the new canals (phase 2), and then connectivity in the form of Green Routes in and out of the city (phase 3) before adding and expanding with new Buildings (phase 4).

14. ESTABLISH HIGH QUALITY ROUTES TO THE WATERFRONT

Make sure that the waterfront is easy to get to and from by establishing a multitude of attractive routes leading down to the water.

15. INVITE PEOPLE TO POPULATE THE WATERFRONT AT ALL TIMES

In order to order to create a truly vibrant waterfront, activities should take place in the public realm and in the adjacent buildings, as well as being inviting to all during the day, week and year around.

16. INTRODUCE ACTIVITIES RELATED TO THE WATER

Use the opportunity to develop water-related activities that supplement existing activities within the city.

17. CREATE DIVERSE SPATIAL EXPERIENCES ALONG THE WATERFRONT

Provide a variety of spaces that accommodate different uses and experiences along the water-front. Develop urban as well as landscape qualities within these spaces.

18. INVITE EVERYONE

Program and design the public spaces so that they are accessible and inviting for everyone, in order to ensure a lively, inclusive, as well as a tolerant city.

19. CREATE ACTIVITIES AT ALL TIMES

Program the spaces and buildings with both permanent activities and temporary events, so that they are used throughout the day and week, all year around.

20. ENCOURAGE "STAYING" ACTIVITIES

Encourage staying activities by providing a variety of places to sit and rest in the public spaces as well as along the main pedestrian routes.

21. USE DIFFERENT ARCHITECTS TO CREATE VARIED EXPERIENCES

Repetition and lack of architectural hierarchy makes it hard for residents to relate to individual dwellings.

Residents should have the feeling that they are living in a understandable social unit where it is easy to belong. Variation and architectural hierarchy create an exciting, as well as an eventful environment.

22. THE CHIMNEY EFFECT CREATES CURRENCY

To ensure that the canals have a good flow, its important to make them wide when they go into the city and narrow when they go out into the River again.

This way, the so-called chimney effect makes sure that the water is being sucked in to the canals and pulled out again into the river.

23. WATER TURBINES PROVIDE POWER 24/7

By installing several water turbines in the new canals, the illumination of the whole city can be provided by a very low polluting energy source.

24. MAKE A YELLOW PLAN

Make an Illumination plan for the city. It is impor-tant to have good lighting along the river and canal sides, both for visibility, as well as having the feeling of safety at night.

Shifting Currents

**Christoper Fannin
+ HOK Planning Group**

Hong Kong, China

RIVERV
ISLA

HILLSBOROUGH RIVER

HYDE PARK

HILLSBOROUGH
BAY

YBOR CITY

YBOR CHANNEL

TAMPA
WETLAND PARK

COUNTY
ISLAND

CHANNELSIDE
ISLAND

TAMPA
MERIDIAN
WATERS

BLUE CANYON

OWN
ND

CANAL

WATERSIDE
ISLAND

GARRISON CHANNEL

HARBOUR
ISLAND

- ● TAMPA AQUARIUM EXTENSION
- ● CRUISE TERMINAL
- ● CONVENTION CENTRE
- ● WATER SPORTS CENTRE
- ● TAMPA UNIVERSITY
- ● WETLAND PARK
- ● TIDAL PARK
- ● URBAN BEACH
- ● MARINA
- ● CULTURAL BARGES
- ● BIO-DIVERSITY ISLAND
- ● AL FRESCO DINING
- ● WATERFRONT RETAIL
- ● BOAT HOUSES
- ● HYDRAULIC POWER GENERATOR
- ○ WATER STOP

500

0   200' 400'   1000'

N

Tampa 2050. Residents kayak to work through restored mangrove habitats, tourists tour the dramatic waterways; local environmental agencies and universities have created habitat research institutes. Tampa is seen as a global example of intricately linked city design and ecological functions.

Today, however, Tampa's ecology is divorced from a decaying urban fabric. Decades of poor planning and suburban flight have seen Tampa turn its back on its primary resource, its ecology and the Hillsborough River.

Shifting Currents is a design intervention that allows Tampa to reclaim its natural heritage, through a bold reconfiguration of its urban and landscape fabric, introducing new waterways within the urban core.

Inspired by the local intertidal habitats, it sets a new benchmark of urban livability and vibrant economy tapping into local ecology, generating new urban conditions along this new water/land interface; intentionally blurred and overlapping.

Co-habitation –To truly address its current problems, Tampa Bay can no longer see human settlements and natural systems as binary. A new symbiotic co-existence between Tampa Bay's once thriving ecological habitats and urban settlements is born.

Intensification – Using water, the very element that has shaped Tampa, vacant or underutilized parcels within the CBD, are 'washed away' to generate new and compact mixed-use development islands, resulting in increased density and waterfront exposure that will lure people and investors back.

Resilience – Mimicking local intertidal ecologies in the way it functions, the city is imbued with a resilience, allowing it to adapt to current and future challenges be they environmental, economic or social.

These principles provide a unique roadmap for Tampa, neither limited in scope, nor modest in its ambitions. To face the challenges Tampa faces today, half of the measures will not achieve the change required. Shifting Currents sets out a bold framework that will position Tampa for the future that it deserves.

INTRODUCTION

For the most part, the coastal cities of North America and Europe are at a point within their development arc where they are not currently experiencing the major population shifts or surges in infrastructure development like that currently seen in Asia. Current changes within these cities and regions are focused, to a large extent, on addressing the issues of decaying infrastructure, as well as reclaiming post-industrial zones that have closed or moved elsewhere, or taking the first steps to adapt to future climate-based events.

Although the threat of climate and sea level change is universal, the implications it raises, the contexts within which it will unfold or is unfolding and, critically, the factors influencing on-the-ground development in the present moment are drastically different and require diverse, multifaceted and fluid responses depending on a projects specific location.

Unlike in many Western cities and regions, the dramatic and rapid shifts in rural to urban population balances, governmental structure and socio-economic structure currently unfolding within the Asia region cannot be overstated. The resulting effects including rapid development, loss of ecological habitat, environmental degradation and even patterns of use within existing or new open spaces require a fundamentally different approach to design. While connections can be drawn between many of these shifts and their contribution to climate change, the issues are, largely, viewed and addressed as being distinct from one another. The immense pressures placed on cities by the aforementioned changes and, ultimately, on local government officials and developers, often mean that the specific issue of climate change and its attendant implications is often not on the table at all.

The unique challenge and opportunity of designing within this rapidly evolving region and on an often large scale has been that, unlike in Western cities, the opportunity exists within Asia to synchronize the design of climate adaptive design strategies with large-scale city building and new infrastructure initiatives – this within a region that, driven by necessity, has a seemingly limitless appetite for large-scale infrastructure projects. Doing so effectively, however, involves an intimate understanding of both macro level policies and priorities, as well as site/regional level ecological systems; it also requires an ability to carefully weave together these often competing ideologies and agendas to synthesize a broadly supported approach, which allows for much-needed development to take place within a sustainable framework/foundation.

The focus of this essay is the topic of waterfront redevelopment and urban resilience, but from a different global perspective. For the Hong Kong-based Planning team of HOK, the (Re) Stitch competition offered an opportunity to test ideas and strategies, which had been refined and applied on a series of large-scale coastal projects across the Asia Pacific region.

Through three very different project examples, we aim to summarize many of the core challenges faced in the Asia Pacific region when embarking on these large scale waterfront redevelopment projects, the lessons learned and, in some cases, the analysis of the successes and failures of the final built environment and, specifically, how these were ultimately applied to the (Re) Stitch Tampa competition.

Tamar Redevelopment, Hong Kong

In 2008, as part of the successful culmination of an international design competition that would see Hong Kong reclaim and redefine the most prominent area of its historic Central Waterfront, the design team, having received input from a multitude of public and private stakeholders involved in this high-profile project, set out a series of idealized design principles, which were intended to function as the underpinning narrative for the project. These were: The Door is Always Open, The Land is Always Green, The Sky will be Blue, and People will be Connected.

These guiding principles, while very broad in scope and potentially vague to those not familiar with the city, were in fact powerful statements intended to tap into underlying emotions within the public and form part of a clear and palatable narrative which spoke to a very broad set of deep-seated desires within the local population. Some, such as The People will be Connected, were more concrete than others and more easily defined in spatial or design terms, while others such as The Sky will be Blue, were harder to pin down in design terms and were in many ways more philosophical.

For this reason, the Tamar Project is a unique example of a large-scale waterfront redevelopment project in that it rests at a very interesting point where landscape is used as both a physical canvas and a metaphor for many broad and idealized goals and philosophical aspirations.

The trajectory the site took to get to its present day form is very compelling and in itself reflects the diverse history and often-competing priorities of the city. Functioning as a naval base during Colonial rule, shifts in policy combined with a growing desire for developable land saw the site and its surrounding areas in an almost constant state of flux, as the city – hungry for developable land – saw a fairly rapid infill of portions of its iconic waterfront which, despite its historic and defining character within the city, was both championed and bemoaned by different sectors of the population. Over time, the site transitioned to an area which is today home to a complex mix of high-density

offices, public sector buildings and commercial development, all connected via a dense and high-capacity network of highways, subways and elevated pedestrian walkways, and all hemmed in between the steep mountains to the south, and Victoria Harbor to the north.

Given the development pressures placed on the Tamar site, combined with the contentious decision to use it as the site of the new Government Headquarters, Tamar is, first and foremost, about providing both a cornerstone for a new public and pedestrian-focused open space along the waterfront and, at a site scale, a platform for citizens to engage with their government. In an interesting twist, this relatively new landscape typology for the city was envisioned and developed at a time of fledgling and often tense political discourse between the local government and its citizens and, at a broader level, amid a desire for an expansion of democratic freedoms from the Central Communist Party in Beijing.

This overarching vision for the open space was also intended to sit neatly on the back of what were several different, overlapping and complex waterfront and transportation infrastructure projects. The desire to use landscape as a green canvas to be stretched over certain elements such as sunken highways and new subway lines, while at the same time acting as connective tissue between other nodes and transportation hubs, provided the project with a far richer and more complex approach to waterfront planning. By defining a very clear and public edge to what had always been a largely inaccessible stretch of waterfront, the design had the added benefit of defining a high-water line for development along this edge and thereby preserving what is a historic and iconic waterfront from further infill.

Judged purely from the point of view of integrating complex infrastructure projects seamlessly within a pedestrian friendly open space, which provide the city with a new waterfront in what was previously inaccessible private land, it is a tremendous success – especially given where it could have gone, given the

pressures from the development community. However, looked at from the more visionary and philosophical point of view, it is unclear how successfully it navigated and solved the more complex issues of sky blue, land green. Many of these issues speak to broader goals and concerns, which, ultimately, the landscape alone will not be able to solve. The landscape has, most critically, provided the stage upon which the discussions and interaction over these issues and others can occur.

How do you judge the ultimate success of a project like the Tamar Redevelopment or compare it to other waterfront redevelopment projects? This is not an easy question to answer. Given the complexity and multi-dimensionality of the project, it cannot be looked at through only one lens and, when compared to other waterfront redevelopment projects both within the region and in other parts of the world, it is clear that it is an interesting hybrid of a purely infrastructure focused project, a waterfront redevelopment and part of a bigger statement about the interaction between a government and its people.

Bringing Eco-tourism to the City: Bandar Seri Begawan, Brunei

The Development Master Plan undertaken for Bandar Seri Begawan represents a participatory, multi-disciplinary approach to how a city with an emerging urban population can mitigate climate risks, while simultaneously accommodating growth, and indeed, promoting economic development within the framework of a healthy and functioning ecosystem.

Located on the northern tip of the Island of Borneo, Brunei, and its most densely populated and urban district, Bandar Seri Begawan (BSB), exists within an area of incredibly rich biodiversity. Historically, the Brunei and Kedayan rivers around which BSB grew, were an integral part of this broader ecosystem and provided vital transportation, economic and ecological functions for the city as well as an extension of the natural habitat. Floating/Water-based communities such as Kampung Ayer, one of the earliest settlements of Brunei and a functioning community today, evolved in a symbiotic relationship with the surrounding environment and provided the city with a unique identity. As the city grew and residents moved inland, the relationship with the local ecology and waterfront changed, with traditional patterns of development making way for typologies, which were disconnected, and at odds with the natural environment.

Over time, Brunei effectively turned its back on this part of its ecological and development history. Many portions of the river were either canalized, stripped of their original biodiversity or simply damaged by the encroachment of the relatively unchecked growth of the surrounding city. The mouth of the rivers became used only as a stepping-off point for eco-focused tours, which quickly leave the city boundaries to immerse tourists within the diverse ecologies within which Bandar Seri Begawan once grew. The result of this neglect was a dying river and a city divorced from the ecological habitat and the functions that the river provided, leaving vast portions of the city at risk of flooding during storm events and surges in water levels.

In early 2010, the Government of Brunei, acting on many of the initiatives outlined in earlier agreements and studies, engaged HOK as the chief author of the new Development Master Plan for Bandar Seri Begawan. Using a participatory approach which, while familiar in many western planning processes, was relatively new to Brunei, the consultant team consisting of planners, biologists, landscape architects and engineers engaged members of the public, businesses leaders and local government through a series of community outreach sessions and workshops in an effort to map out concerns and develop strategies which would work at both a policy and community level.

At the heart of the final proposed development plan is a series of strategies that would not only deal with present day and future fluctuations in water levels and damaging storm events through sensitively designed solutions, but also strategies that would simultaneously restore and embrace lost ecologies, celebrate the Bruneian identity, and help to build a more sustainable and diverse foundation for the city's future growth and economic progress.

However, perhaps the key principle driving the Development Master Plan is the philosophical and also physical re-connecting of the growing capital city with its greatest asset – its ecological and cultural heritage. The rainforests surrounding the city, threatened by encroaching development, and the city's rivers, long polluted and forgotten, are to be revitalized and indeed are intended to become the focus of the city's future. The strategies included:

– Establishing a "riverfront eco-corridor" along the Kedayan River to protect wetland and mangrove ecologies, which are instrumental in absorbing and mitigating impacts of water surge/storm events and associated pollution runoff.

– Using native plant species and mangroves to re-establish a continuous riverfront ecology, which in turn would encourage return of the native wildlife species that foster the region's eco-tourism economy.

– Defining a series of urban, sub-urban and natural waterfront edge conditions, with associated land uses and development densities, which would allow the restored river ecology to co-exist peacefully with the city.

– Integrating a sensitively designed system of riverside pathways and trails, which would allow residents and tourists alike to access this previously off-limits or degraded resource. A water taxi system was also put in place to provide additional means of accessing different points and attractions along the river as well as providing alternative public transportation.

– In addition to riverside bunds and restored river edges, a series of flood resilience parks were designed or retrofitted within existing parks that were adjacent to the river. These systems, in collaboration with the river and the citywide infrastructure, would help to alleviate future flooding problems.

– Careful attention was paid to local use patterns and architectural qualities and these were sensitively integrated into the design to ensure a level of comfort.

– Where applicable, development both within and adjacent to the river in the form of eco-resorts, riverfront restaurants and pedestrian promenades was encouraged as a way to enable more sustainable forms of economic growth within riverfront corridors.

– Focusing development in "action areas" and encouraging more compact development, rather than allowing urban sprawl at the city's edges, enabled by the annexation of hinterlands into Bandar Seri Begawan's municipal boundary. The preservation of rainforest canopy alone can help to absorb rainfall and reduce runoff by 20%.

With these strategies, the Development Master Plan attempts to shape a growing city into one that is both resilient to climate change but also productive, and to do so, it depends heavily on supporting its various ecosystems – treating them not as external to the city, but as part of it. The goal for Bandar Seri Begawan is a human settlement that enhances local ecology by functioning at least as well as a healthy, high-functioning Borneo lowland rainforest.

A Facelift for a 'Garden City': Lovers' Road Redevelopment, Zhuhai, China

Zhuhai is relatively new albeit strategically important when compared with many of China's cities. It was brought into existence in 1980 as one of the original Special Economic Zones (SEZ) created by the Chinese Central Government as a means of spurring development within an important part of the country. Its location, directly opposite the Special Administrative Region (SAR) of Macau, and within close proximity to both Hong Kong and Guangzhou (China's third largest city with 8.5 million residents), along with its broad range of newly built supporting infrastructure, contributed to a population and development boom.

Geographically, Zhuhai is located at the confluence of the Pearl River Delta and the South China Sea; a sub-tropical zone which supports a rich marine ecology along with economically important shipping industries. Made up of approximately 146 islands and with a coastline stretching to 690km, Zhuhai has positioned itself as a popular beachside holiday destination.

The growing coastal-focused tourism industry, coupled with a rapidly growing urban population, a large proportion of which lives and plays within very close proximity to the delta, has given rise to an urgency to address the need for development overall, especially the creation of public open spaces and supporting infrastructure, and to find ways to cope with the fallout from seasonal flooding due to the typhoons common during the summer months.

In 2009, faced with growing pressures originating from its rapid growth and expansion, the Government launched a design competition aimed at generating redevelopment strategies for a 50km stretch of Lovers' Road – a famous coastal road that traverses a broad cross-section of Zhuhai's urban and waterfront fabric. Given the context, the parameters the design had to address were diverse and, as the winner of the competition, HOK was tasked with tackling the conceptual and detailed design for the first phase, which included 18km of streetscapes and 9 ha of new or redeveloped waterfront parks.

Within this context, the Lovers' Road Redevelopment is best viewed as the physical manifestation of several interconnected and overlapping local, regional and national priorities. At a regional and national scale, the Zhuhai waterfront is the entry and exit point in a massive infrastructure project cwurrently under construction that will see Zhuhai, Hong wKong and Macau connected by a 50km long series of tunnels and elevated highways spanning the South China Sea. Slated for completion in 2016, this project will further link these cities both physically and economically to other urban centers within Guangdong province. At a city level, it involved addressing issues of identity and branding, as the city saw the new and improved waterfront as playing a critical role in projecting Zhuhai's dynamic urban face toward Macau, seen by many as the glitzier and wealthier neighbor, just a few hundred meters across the channel. At a community level, it involved finding a balance between the demands for additional developable land and the resulting need for expanded open space for the rapidly growing local population. Finally, at a site-specific level, it is a response to the need for improved storm surge protection along the exposed portions of the waterfront, which typically suffer from localized flooding during the annual typhoon season.

Given the multi-layered complexity of the project, the ultimate success of the design response rested heavily on the team having a clear understanding of the both the macro and micro level priorities as a means of aligning the diverse and often competing interests of both individuals and organizations with the primary requirements of the site. While time-consuming, this strategy ensured that the longer-term interest and performance criteria of the site were not shortchanged against the immediate requirements of the shorter-term interests. Examples of this were found within the adaptive reuse of existing waterfront infrastructure as much-needed new public waterfront amenity spaces,

and also the creation of a series of large terraced parks that form a new resilient green barrier against the seasonal typhoons which batter the coastline and typically cause extensive flooding. Both of these strategies accomplished these goals while at the same time addressing calls for new developable land as well as an expanded and, in parts, integrated highway infrastructure.

The design opportunities and challenges that were present within this particular context are representative of both the enormous scope and ambitions of many of the waterfront redevelopment initiatives currently underway in the region. What was particularly unique within this context was the way that landscape occupied the intersection between policy, branding and ecology. Within this particular case, it was not enough for the design to simply address one single challenge – such as meeting the need for existing and future growth, or providing a solution for environmental problems, or projecting an image of a city's vision for

itself. The final design, in order to be successful on all levels, had to create a structure that addressed a very wide range of different but interconnected challenges, one that provided the platform for the city's future sustainable growth and offered its inhabitants a vibrant and harmonious environment.

CONCLUSION

The lessons offered by the three case studies highlighted within this essay – redeveloping the Tamar Government Headquarters in Hong Kong, the densely populated and urban district of Bandar Seri Begawan in Brunei and the coastal Lovers' Road in Zhuhai, China – are extremely diverse, and reflect not only the well-documented scale and pace of change within the Asia Pacific region but, more importantly, a willingness to tackle a broad range of complex issues under the banner of what are typically seen as fairly generic, top-down waterfront infrastructure projects.

All of these projects have embraced landscape in its broadest sense as a mechanism for more effectively re-engaging cities and their inhabitants with their local ecology, government or urban fabric, while at the same time solving very pressing and timely issues of flooding/storm events, growing infrastructure and projecting an effective image. This essay has highlighted how landscape can be used very effectively to fulfill important requirements in cities across the region, and there are of course many other examples demonstrating this theme across the region that could be discussed. While it is true that many Asian cities and parts of the regions sit at a very different point in their development arc when compared to their North American or European counterparts, the lessons they offer both in terms of the scope and scale are high relevant, if not always directly transferrable, given the current focus on re-inhabiting, restoring or strengthening our waterfronts.

Symbiosis Ri-verizing Tampa

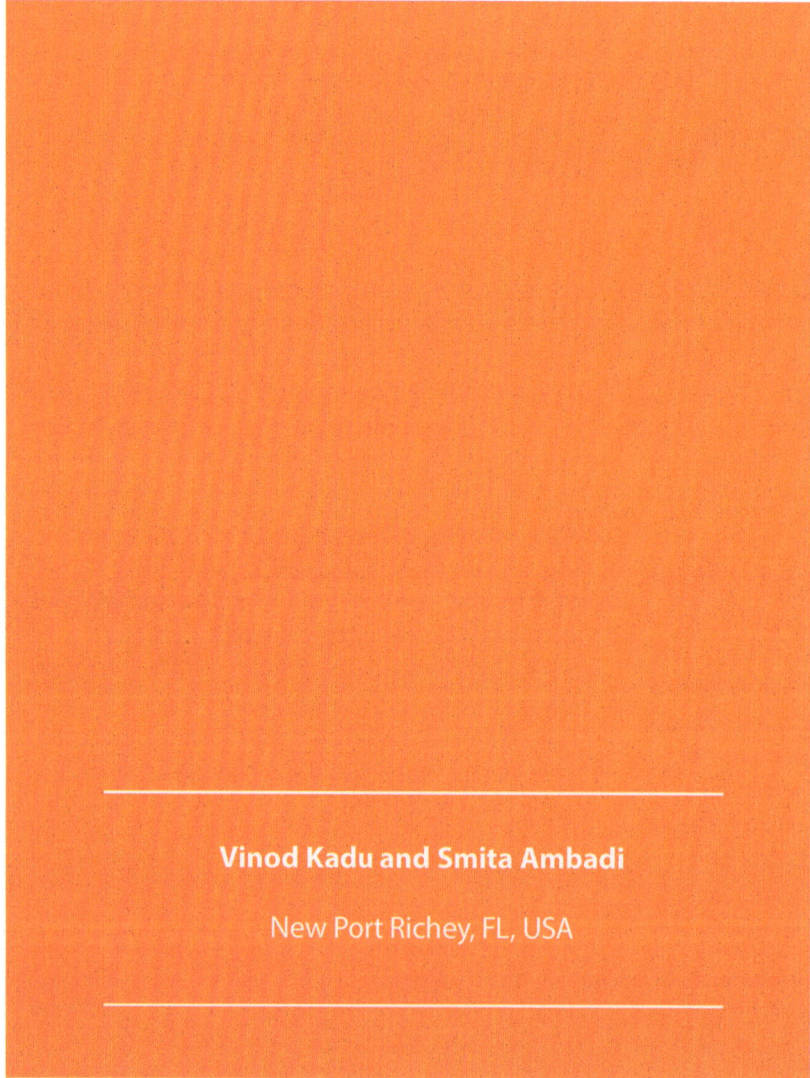

Vinod Kadu and Smita Ambadi

New Port Richey, FL, USA

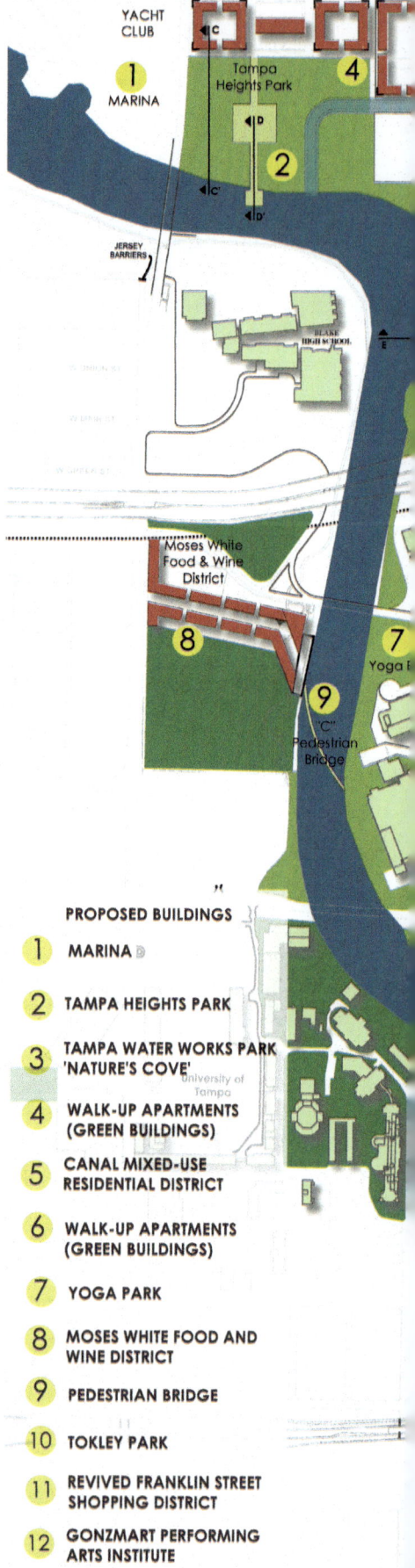

PROPOSED BUILDINGS

1. MARINA
2. TAMPA HEIGHTS PARK
3. TAMPA WATER WORKS PARK 'NATURE'S COVE'
4. WALK-UP APARTMENTS (GREEN BUILDINGS)
5. CANAL MIXED-USE RESIDENTIAL DISTRICT
6. WALK-UP APARTMENTS (GREEN BUILDINGS)
7. YOGA PARK
8. MOSES WHITE FOOD AND WINE DISTRICT
9. PEDESTRIAN BRIDGE
10. TOKLEY PARK
11. REVIVED FRANKLIN STREET SHOPPING DISTRICT
12. GONZMART PERFORMING ARTS INSTITUTE

5

11

10

Tokley Park

ELEVATED SELMON CROSSTOWN EXPRESSWAY

LEE ROY SELMON CROSSTOWN EXPRESSWAY

LEE ROY SELMON CROSSTOWN EXPRESSWAY

Tampa Fire
Dept.

Tampa
Firefighter's
Museum

RAMPELLO
SCHOOL

THE FLORIDA
AQUARIUM

Existing Landmarks/
Points of Interest

Church/Open Space/ Libraries

Gateway

Tampa - Core Downtown
Function

Main Auto-oriented Routes

Esplanade/Tampa Riverwalk

Tampa Canalwalk

Proposed Routes enhancing
pedestrian movement from
Origin to Destination

Tampa Canal District

Proposed High Density
Mixed use Residential

Existing High Density Mixed Use
Residential Development near
Channel District

Proposed Revival of Franklin
Street as High Density Residential
and Retail on First Floor

Proposed Tampa Cultural
District - Theatre, Food & Wine

Movement of People from
Neighboring Districts

SYMBIOSIS

The Hillsborough River is a great asset to the City of Tampa. Although it has a lot to offer it, the river currently flows through the city as, almost a complete stranger. The intention of this design is to turn the city around, shift the focus back to the river, and to create opportunities to befriend it. This design treats the river as a catalyst for change. Its intention is to capture the advantages afforded by the proximity to this dynamic natural element. The concept is to explore and enjoy the multiple benefits that the river has to offer, and in return, understand its needs and give back the care and respect that it deserves. The design uses the river as the key element to solve some of the current issues, create opportunities for today and tomorrow, and to establish the capacity to deal with future needs.

The design addresses these multiple agendas by focusing on three key strategies:

-Connecting to the river
-Getting to know the river and
-Building a long lasting sustainable relationship with it

Open Space adjacent to Canal
Landscaped for community use

15 Ft.
Canalwalk

30 Ft.
Canal Width Under Bridge

15 Ft.
Canalwalk

Open Space adjacent to Canal
Landscaped for community use

Connections with the river are established by bringing people to the river or bringing the river into the urban environs. Extending the city to the waterfront is achieved by extending the physical and visual connections to the river, and creating a ring of destination points located at walkable distances from the river's edge. These destinations will attract footfalls and bring people closer to the river, while the visual and physical connections, and the supporting bike and pedestrian infrastructure, will help extend these visits to the river. The extension of the river and nature to the heart of downtown in the form of the proposed Canal is another unique feature that will benefit the residents, shoppers, and businesses alike. The intention is to create a system that not just introduces the experience of nature deep into downtown, but that also creates an integrated sustainable system of storm water management, flood protection, microclimate generation, as well as recreation.

The design further reinforces the connection to the river by creating a continuous esplanade dotted by unique destination points at walkable distances. The proposed convergence of nature and urban environ-ments along the riverfront creates tremendous opportunities for economic growth, aesthetic and visual pleasure, entertainment, recreation, education, as well as spiritual healing. The design captures and embraces the dynamic nature of water and creates unique destinations portraying diverse-friendly and mutually beneficial-ways of engaging with nature. By doing this, it successfully connects to a wide range of Tampa's users such as: residents, tourists, downtown employees, students, families, children, and others -offering something for everyone. Some of the proposed functions such as the yoga deck, Neighborhood Park, and esplanade also help to re-establish the Hillsborough River as an integral part of the health and lifestyle of Tampa's residents. Overall this design combines the key ingredients – connections, ecology, and infrastructure in varying degrees to create a *symbiotic* relationship with the river. A relationship that opens up opportunities for not just correcting some of our past development errors, but also for improving today's quality of life. Furthermore, this design is an attempt to reposition the City of Tampa to effectively deal with some of the future challenges such as climate change, storm surge, and sea level rise.

Selected Proposals

Streets

Branches of the River

Taekyung Kim, student at
Harvard Graduate School of Design

Cambridge, MA, USA + Seoul, South Corea

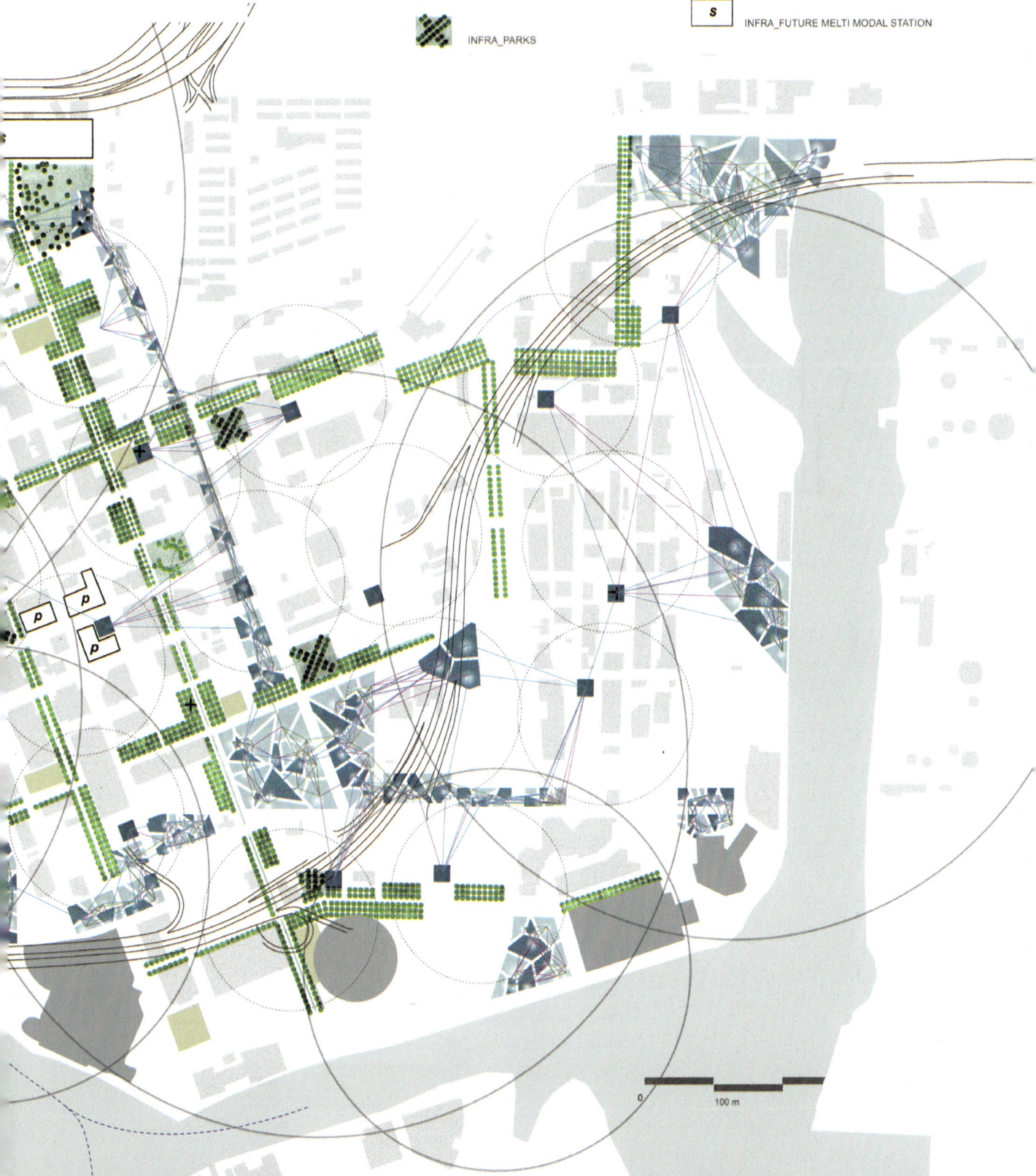

GREEN CORRIDOR

WETLANDS

1ST GREYWATER COLLECTING WETLAND

INFRA_PARKS

INFRA_PUBLIC SQUARE

INFRA_POINTS OF INTEREST

p INFRA_MAJOR PUBLIC PARKING LOT

s INFRA_FUTURE MELTI MODAL STATION

0   100 m

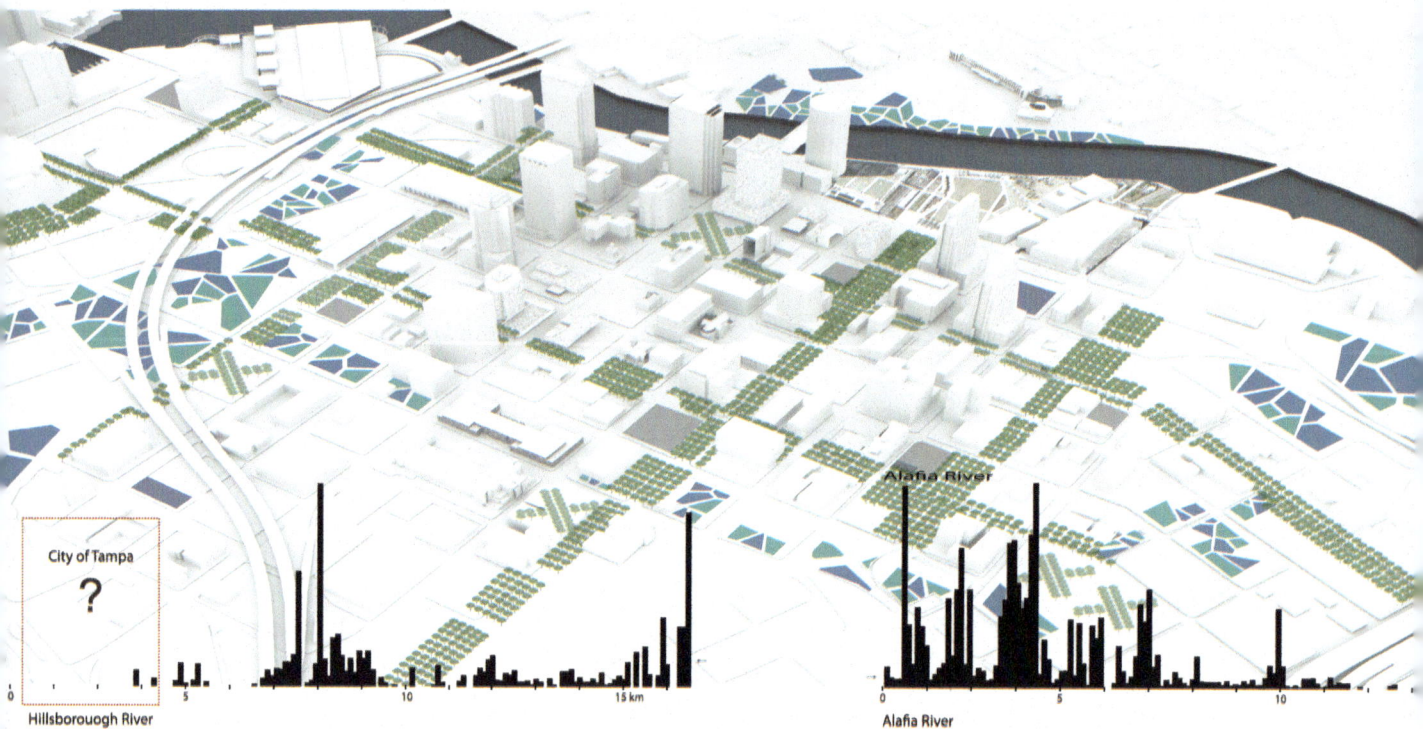

City of Tampa
?

Hillsborouogh River

Alafia River

Alafia River

1

INTRODUCTION

The Hillsborough River as a major spine, drives this project in the re-vitalizing the City of Tampa. The Riverwalk project, as well as Curtis Hixon Park and many interesting points located throughout the river are already making the river an active urban infrastructure. The lower Hillsborough River edge, however, has almost no ecological features as compared to the nearby Alafia River. The Hillsborough River possessed more potential in the city than it does now. This project is initiated from the conception that not only is the river and its function experienced right at its geographical location, but that its function is also experienced on the way to the river. The value of the river, as well as its hydrological and ecological functions are all extended into the city, as are its cultural and economic drivers. Therefore, "The Street" exists not only as the pathway to reach the river, but as a tributary or branch(es) of the river itself. Economy, culture, and hydrological systems will be overlaid onto the street systems, thus connecting to the river. Finally, the streets will be transformed as contextual branches of the river. These branches will ecologically revitalize the river's edge. Subsequently, the transformation of Tampa's street corridors will reveal the blue print of the strategic planning strategy of the City of Tampa.

GREEN CORRIDOR

WETLANDS

1ST GREYWATER COLLECTING WETLAND

INFRA_PARKS

INFRA_PUBLIC SQUARE

INFRA_POINTS OF INTEREST

p   INFRA_MAJOR PUBLIC PARKING LOT

s   INFRA_FUTURE MELTI MODAL STATION

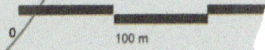

0   100 m

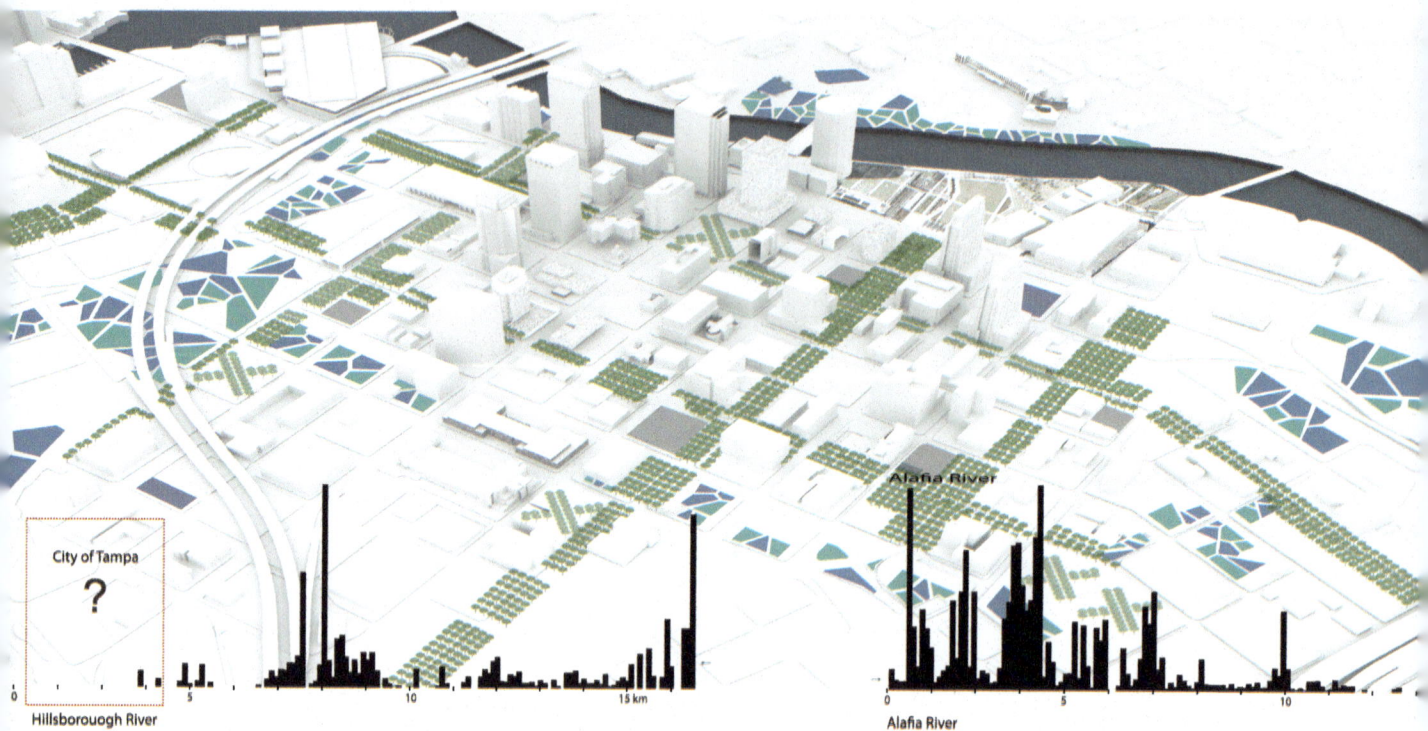

City of Tampa
?

Hillsborouogh River

Alafia River

1

INTRODUCTION

The Hillsborough River as a major spine, drives this project in the re-vitalizing the City of Tampa. The Riverwalk project, as well as Curtis Hixon Park and many interesting points located throughout the river are already making the river an active urban infrastructure. The lower Hillsborough River edge, however, has almost no ecological features as compared to the nearby Alafia River. The Hillsborough River possessed more potential in the city than it does now. This project is initiated from the conception that not only is the river and its function experienced right at its geographical location, but that its function is also experienced on the way to the river. The value of the river, as well as its hydrological and ecological functions are all extended into the city, as are its cultural and economic drivers. Therefore, "The Street" exists not only as the pathway to reach the river, but as a tributary or branch(es) of the river itself. Economy, culture, and hydrological systems will be overlaid onto the street systems, thus connecting to the river. Finally, the streets will be transformed as contextual branches of the river. These branches will ecologically revitalize the river's edge. Subsequently, the transformation of Tampa's street corridors will reveal the blue print of the strategic planning strategy of the City of Tampa.

PHASE-1. UNDULATING THE RIVER'S EDGE

The project began from the identification, as well as the generation of critical points which addressed the competition design challenge. We began by taking the current positive conditions existing within the city: river walk planning and points of interest. Through the softening of several spots along the river's edge, both the ecological, as well as the cultural features of the Hillsborough River will be diversified from its current homogenous hard-edged development. Additionally, it was proposed that across the urban fabric that small-sized wetlands would be located in order to deal with greywater. These wetlands located both along softened river edges, as well as across the city, will create its own urban water watershed and function within the urban hydrological system in the future.

PHASE-2. BRANCHING THE RIVER

The ecological as well as the hydrological contexts of the river are extended into streets. Green corridors are vitalized as cultural pedestrian-friendly streets located under an urban forest canopy. They treat urban storm water with Best Management Practices (BMP), and the locations are carefully selected within the urban context like Franklin Street. Blue corridors pass through the urban fabric, connecting river edge wetlands to the city. These act as major corridors where greywater is treated within a large portion of the constructed wetlands. These two corridors enhance the ecological, cultural and hydrological connections with the city and the river.

PHASE-3. URBAN NODES

River, Green, Blue, mobile corridors generate their own narratives within the city. People, vehicles and water will flow along these corridors. Its crossing points are also important transition or gathering spots for them. These crossing points will introduce basic urban infrastructures like squares, parks, wetlands, as well as existing points of interest and parking lots based on used different types and typologies generated from intersected corridors.

VISION FOR THE CITY OF TAMPA

The project transforms urban streets into infrastructure which links existing urban landmarks, as well as creating additional cultural urban nodes by the integrating a new layer of ecology over the existing urban fabric. Ecological corridors will promote the quality and quantity of emergent aquatic vegetation of the Lower Hillsborough River, which one is barely aware of in its current state. Simultaneously, new urban crossing points will be developed which extend the cultural experiences of the city towards the river.

2

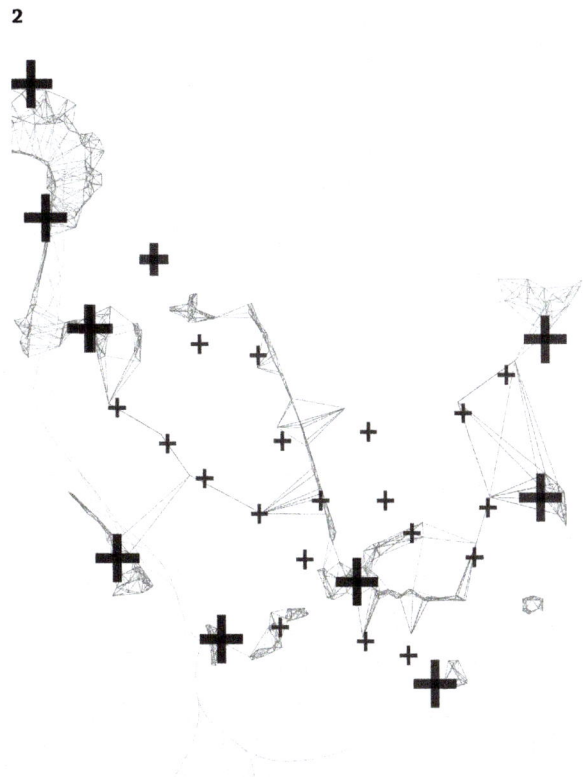

STORMWATER TREATMENT

○ Stormwater watershed
- - → Surface Runoff
↔ Bioswale
◯ Floodplain Wetlands
▾ Output to the river

P S

Legend:
- GREEN CORRIDOR
- WETLANDS
- 1ST GREYWATER COLLECTING WETLAND
- INFRA_PARKS
- INFRA_PUBLIC SQUARE
- INFRA_POINTE OF INTEREST
- P INFRA_MAJOR PUBLIC PARKING LOT
- S INFRA_FUTURE MELTI MODAL STATION

0   100 m   500 m

100 year flood (+8')
high tide (+4')
average (0')
low tide (-3')

| EXISTING RIVER EDGE | RIVER | LOW MARSH | HIGH MARSH | | FLOOD PLAIN |

brackish water flow
average tide ↓   average tide ↓   hightide ↓   hightide ↓

| EXTENDED RIVER EDGE | RIVER | TIDAL FLAT ISLAND | LITTORAL WETLANDS | TIDAL FLAT | LOW MARSH | HIGH MARSH ISLAND |

fresh water flow
over flow ↓   over flow ↓   over flow ↓

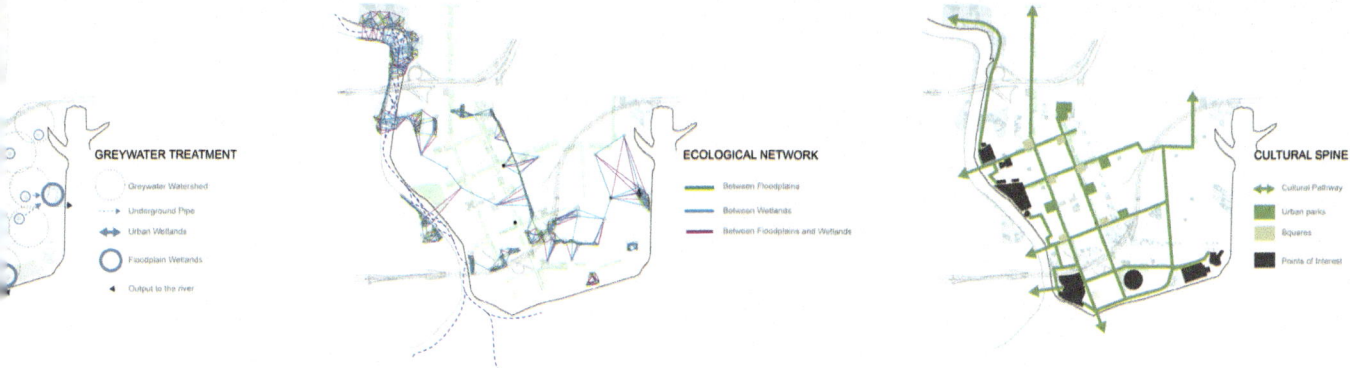

GREYWATER TREATMENT

- Greywater Watershed
- Underground Pipe
- Urban Wetlands
- Floodplain Wetlands
- Output to the river

ECOLOGICAL NETWORK

- Between Floodplains
- Between Wetlands
- Between Floodplains and Wetlands

CULTURAL SPINE

- Cultural Pathway
- Urban parks
- Squares
- Points of Interest

DESIGN CRITERIA. VITALIZING THE EDGES

RIVER EDGE = CITY + RIVER

CURRENT   THICKENING   UNDULATING

URBAN EDGE = BUILDING + STREET

CURRENT   THICKENING   UNDULATING

GREEN CORRIDOR

BUILDING TYPOLOGY. high density with 1st floor retail / setback + inlet

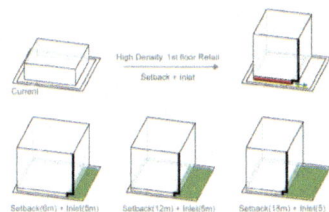

Current

High Density 1st floor Retail
Setback + inlet

Setback(6m) + Inlet(5m)   Setback(12m) + Inlet(5m)   Setback(18m) + Inlet(5)

HYDRO CIRCULATION. stormwater treatment

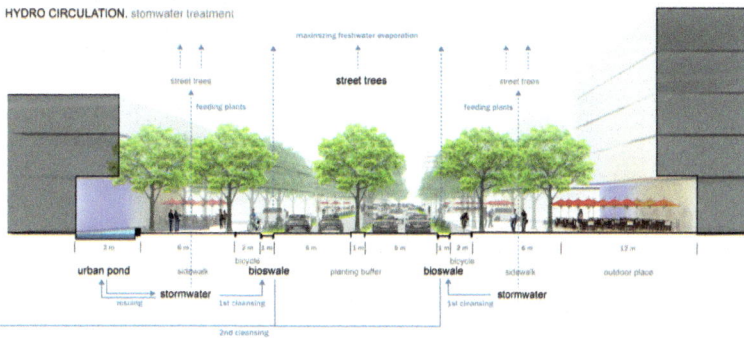

maximizing freshwater evaporation

street trees   street trees   street trees
feeding plants   feeding plants

2 m | 6 m | 2 m | 3 m | 6 m | 1 m | 6 m | 3 m | 2 m | 6 m | 17 m

urban pond   sidewalk   bicycle   bioswale   planting buffer   bioswale   bicycle   sidewalk   outdoor place

reusing → stormwater   1st cleansing   1st cleansing   stormwater

2nd cleansing

BLUE CORRIDOR

BUILDING TYPOLOGY. low density with / setback + greenroof

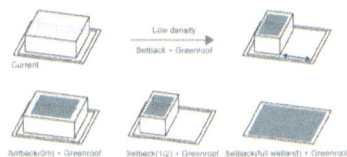

Current

Low density
Setback + Greenroof

Setback(0m) + Greenroof   Setback(1/2) + Greenroof   Setback(full wetland) + Greenroof

HYDRO CIRCULATION. greywater treatment

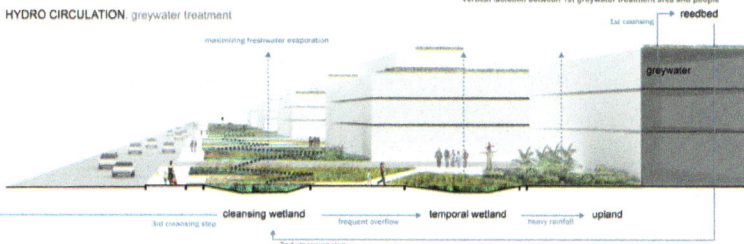

vertical isolation between 1st greywater treatment area and people

1st cleansing → reedbed

maximizing freshwater evaporation

greywater

cleansing wetland   → frequent overflow →   temporal wetland   → heavy rainfall →   upland

1st cleansing step
2nd cleansing step

RIVER EDGE

hightide   coastal flood   coastal flood
| HIGH MARSH | FLOOD PLAIN | FLOOD PLAIN WETLAND | FLOOD PLAIN | UPLAND URBAN WETLAND |
mixed fresh and brackish water   urban water purification   storm / grey water

fresh and brackish water   potential mixing area of fresh and brackish water

Tampa [Eco]Grid

Feriel Mestiri and Xuan Lam Nguyen
(students at Ecole Nationale Superieure d'architecture Paris val de Seine)

Paris, France

Tampa is a city of anomalies, anomalies that must be solved by a critical re-thinking of Tampa's urban structure. These anomalies lie mainly within the implementaion of mono-use zoning, the impact of which has increased and compounded over time, and which has led to the creation of disconnected neighborhoods with heterogeneous activities during the hours of the day. This has included the pheomena of the Central Business District (CBD), which empties out at night, creating an empty district, whereas the bedroom communities of the residential suburbs in the residentially zones areas, welcome its inhabitants.

Despite the city's imbalanced development, the site contains the potential to be a dynamic city that is environmentally friendly.

KEY ELEMENTS COMPOSING THE CITY'S IDENTITY

The river acts as a city geographical center, *the towers:* the vertical density of the city, *the university* as a large green urban space, the left behind *ground parking lots* covering the North-East side of the city and *the highway:* a horizontal plan, floating on top of the city. Each one of these key elements should be studied both as a whole, as well as singular components which work together to create the phenomena that is the City of Tampa.

The discontinuity of the city also comes from *the river* that loops around the whole city. This area is left behind, and remains untapped, especially since it is considered as a border between the shores of both sides.

The towers are mostly located on one side of the river. Today, they are out of scale and they look like stand-alone objects. There is a lack of connection between what people can get as an urban landscape walking around different districts, and this concentric high rise shape as a form of politic, economic and social power which remains detached from the rest of the city.

Transportation activity is intense, especially that of automobiles, which play a predominant role in the city (over 50 percent of the city surface is occupied by parking lots).

The ecosystem that existed around the city tends to

have disappeared. Green spaces are becoming very rare, despite the recent attempts to resolve this issue.

The strong existence of *the aerial auto road* at the North and South side of the city, appears to be a visually disturbing boundary. This infrastructure is, furthermore, more a source of pollution (noise, dirt, vehicle smoke, etc.)

By emphasizing these actual problems of the city, we allow for an understanding of the city's environmental context and identity. The city of Tampa wouldn't exist it without these elements. Efficient and sustainable solutions might be to consider and transform unhealthy features into the potential for an ecological infrastructural proposition.

[ECO]GRID: FROM DISCONTINUITY TO INTERACTION

The competition's charge is framed as a critical re-thinking of Tampa's urban structure by conceptualizing of the river as the spine of the city, as well as focusing on the three major elements of **Ecology, Infrastructure** and **Connectivity.**

Currently, an orthogonal urban grid characterizes the post-war American city, as exemplified by Tampa. We propose an [ECO]GRID, which is super-imposed onto the existing urban grid of Tampa. We usr the city of Amsterdam where the river seeps into the restructured city, as a reference. The urban grid thus overlaps with the Eco-grid.

WHAT MAKES UP THE [ECO]GRID?

The morphology of the Eco-grid is similar to the urban one, although it is less dense because it cannot occupy the entire traffic surface. Its main axes go from East to West and North to South.

Its components are the *platform* and *channels*.

The activities are "green", with the reintroduction of oysters and clams that are inherent to the city's history. The increase in "green" spaces is also an integral part of our plans. The canals will allow for the drainage of rainwater to the river and thus reduce flood risk. Infrastructure is made up of both channels, which allow the reduction of automobile traffic, as well as the promotion of river transport (closer to tourist activities). The platform acts simultaneously as a bridge, a plaza and an observatory over the city. The latter becomes a major activity center, located between the university, the Theater district and the Central Business District. It has space openings for restaurants, as well as a small amphitheater that can be used outside the university. This would give a direct contact with the river's bio-system if necessary, for students.

We are also proposing strategies which are focussed on the separated elements. We looked at them equally, as a whole, and the impact they could have to the environment, according to the daily city life. Indeed, nowadays the use of cars creates more than pollution. Cars have an impact on society; people are more and more isolated in their vehicles. The mode of travelling has changed: there is only the notion of going from place to place by car. The social sustainability, however, should be provided with human exchanges, ways to slow down the life rhythms, and equally a city where people are connected to its accommodations. We can no longer live in a detached site, where the daily circle is from home to work and work to home. There's a need of enjoying the landscape, the public space, the weather, as well as the surrounding activities… The notion of "ecological infrastructure" is an important element with which to begin to transform the city.

HERE IN TAMPA, IT IS ALL ABOUT INFRASTRUCTURE

With the eco-grid, we first began to attempt at decreasing the use of cars. We then focussed on developing the pedestrian possibilities. Finally, we proposed the new channel system as a complement to enrich the experience of living in the City of Tampa. We down-scaled the un-human vastness size of space of the actual environment (where only cars can afford its well function) to more sophisticated sections. Less cars, more walking, more human contacts. More walking means more ground activities, more contemplation and search of the city identity as well as personal interests.

The *[Eco]Grid* is a new layer which is applied onto the existing urban fabric in the search for harmony and relationships of different levels of the society. The quest seems to need profound actions in order to transform such complexity. Indeed, to fulfill the challenge of this scale, it is not simply about figures or shape, but rather, garnering a deep understanding of the historical base, culture and tradition of Tampa.

The proposal belongs to the scale of the study, questioning and testing some capacities of today's environment. We understand the position of different existing parameters of the city. However, in order to reach the different aspects of the urbanization of Tampa and its push towards the potential of new states, a utopian solution is proposed, regardless of its feasibility.

To summarize, the *[Eco]Grid* can bring the city together, cross it on all sides and, most of all. bring the river back to its central position. With the zoning system reduced, underground activities that take place at the canal level, will enable the city to come back to life wherever the canals are, while reconnecting it directly to the river.

[Eco]Grid in the future: extensible and scalable.

As an integrated part of the urban grid, the [ECO]GRID is extensible and scalable. It is a flexible system, that aims to integrate the environment into the city.

FROM DISCONTINUITY TO INTERACTION

ACTIVITIES DISCONECTION

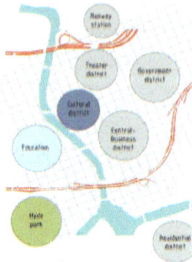

THE RIVER CREATES THE CONNECTION

REPLACING AN EXCESS OF PARKING BY GREEN AND WATER SPACES

ENHANCEMENT OF THE HIGHWAY/ RETHINKING THE TRANSPORTATION

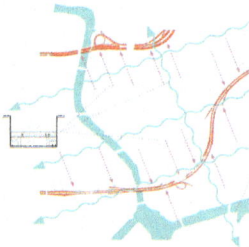

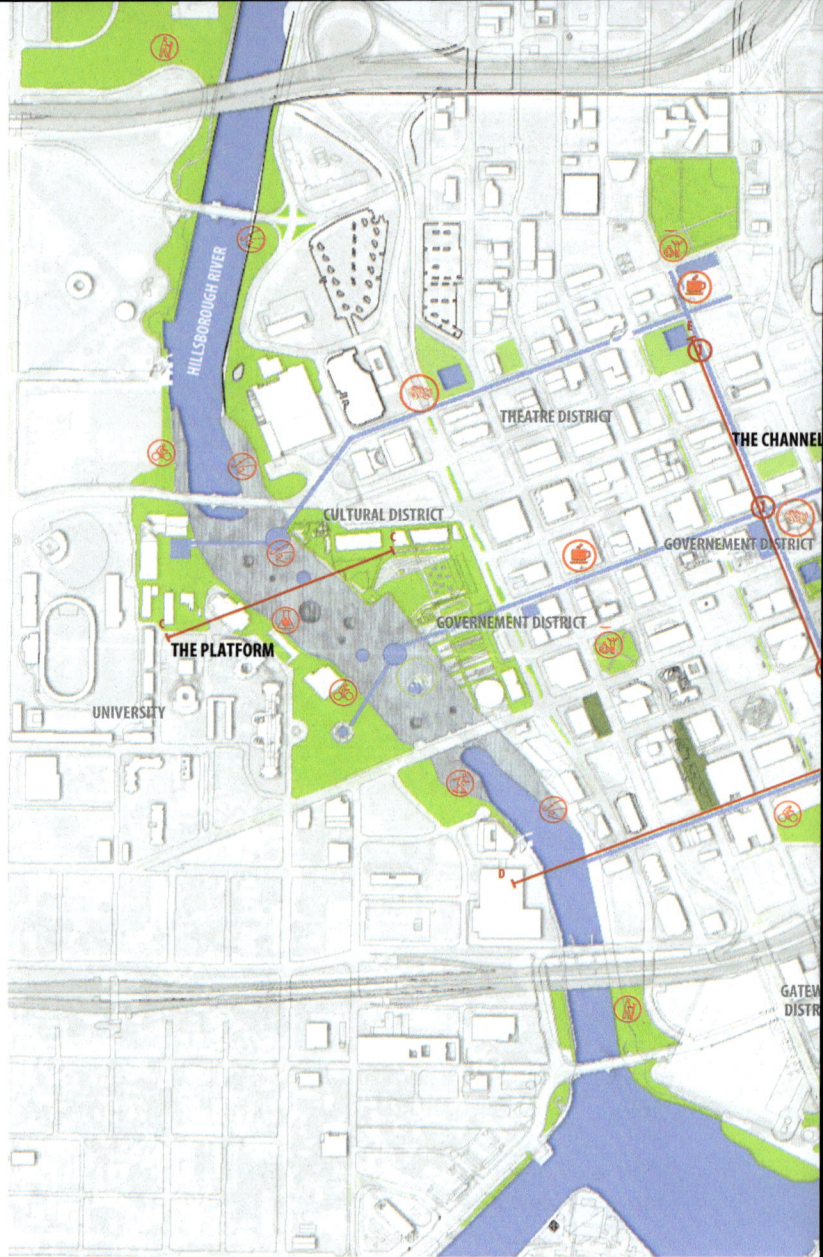

HILLSBOROUGH RIVER

THEATRE DISTRICT

THE CHANNEL

CULTURAL DISTRICT

GOVERNEMENT DISTRICT

THE PLATFORM

GOVERNEMENT DISTRICT

UNIVERSITY

GATEW
DISTR

1

ECOGRID MATER PLAN
Overlapping the city grid with an ecological grid using the river extension as a struc

INFRASTRUCTURE:
Low impact design bringing the river to the city through channels and a plateform

INFRASTRUCTURE

The platform bridge/plaza

Channel

River transportation

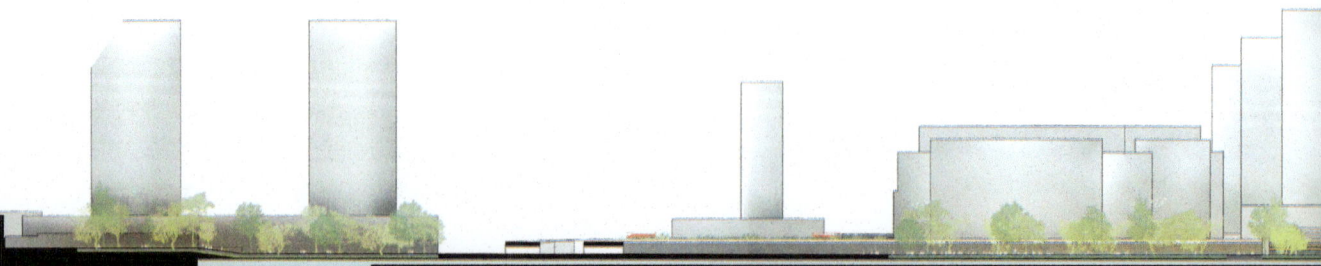

LITTLE TAMPA GARDEN
Large green space aera for enjoying a meal in a natural space

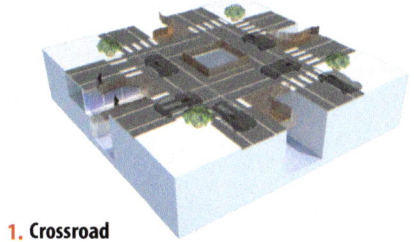

CHANNEL TREATMENT

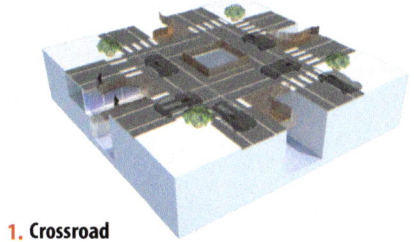

1. Crossroad

WILD PARK
Natural habitat restoration specific to Tampa area.

BIRDS PARK
Birds habitat restoration specific to Tampa area.

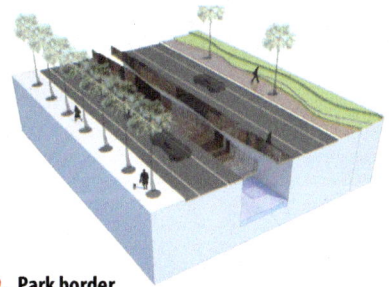

2. Park border

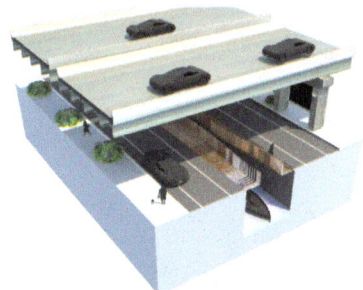

3. Highway intersection

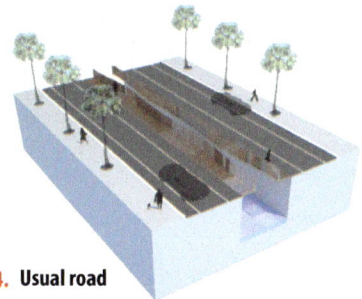

4. Usual road

ECOLOGY:
Reintroducing biodiversity and green spaces
Cleaning river water

CONNECTIVITY:
social activities

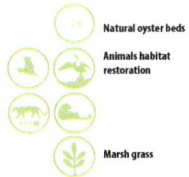

Natural oyster beds

Animals habitat restoration

Marsh grass

Leisures :

Gondola ride

Outside classroom

Hiking

Exercising area

Cycling

Fishing

Food :

Oyester restaurant

Restaurant

Coffee, Bars

Spur on / Spur off

Ecology/Infrastructure/ Connectivity+Economy

Mo Zell-bauenstudio with Keith Hayes

Milwaukee, Wisconsin, USA

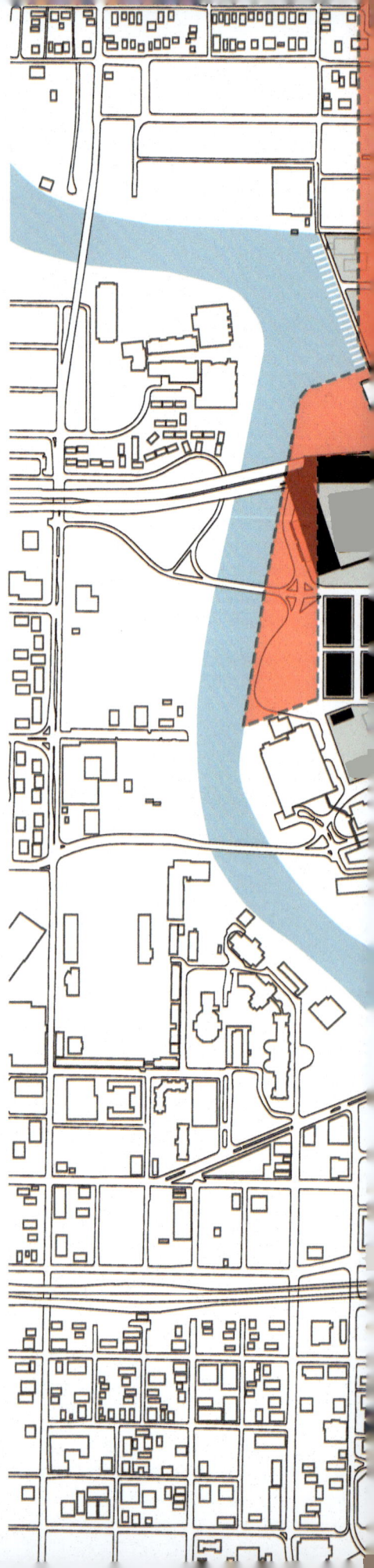

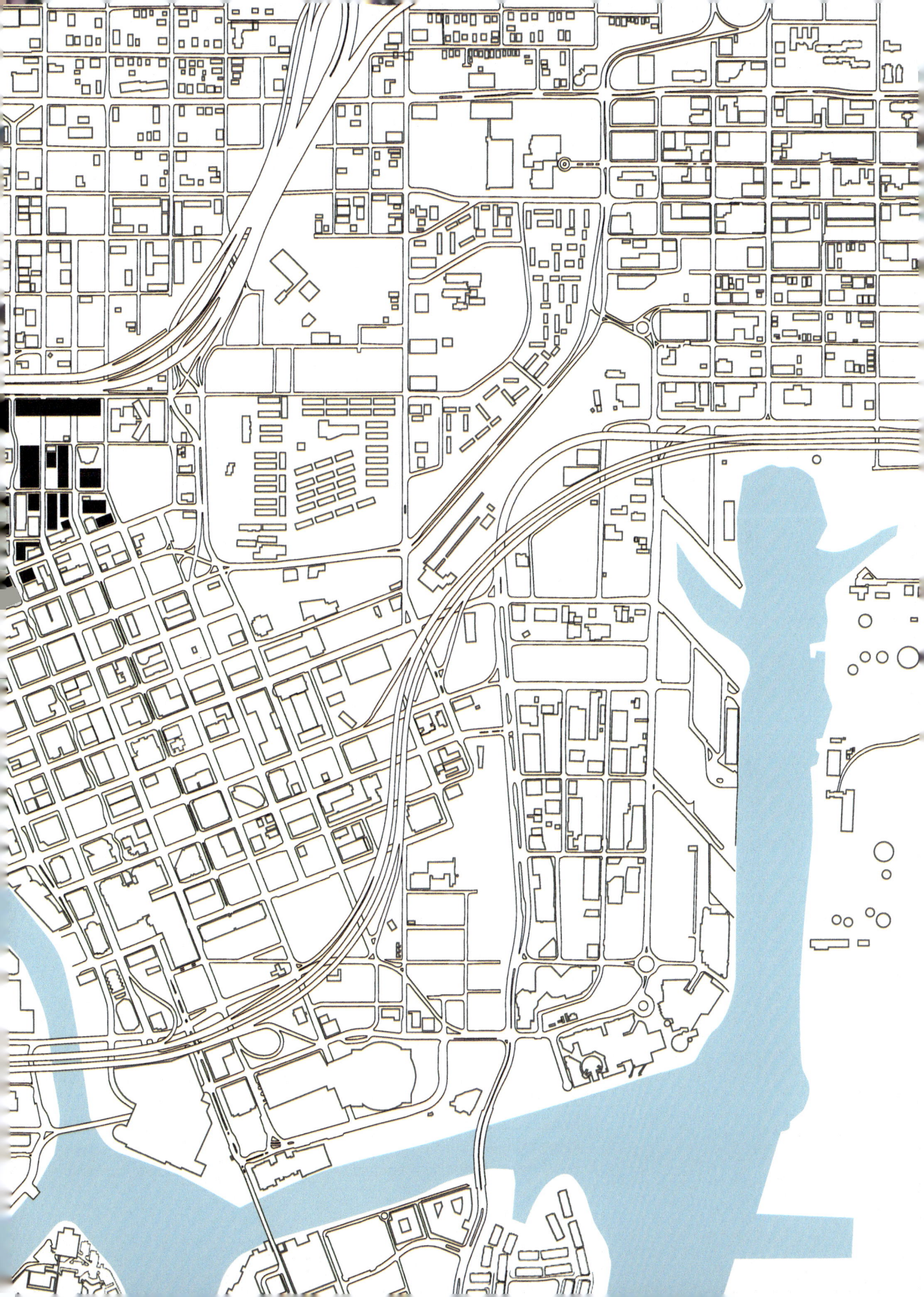

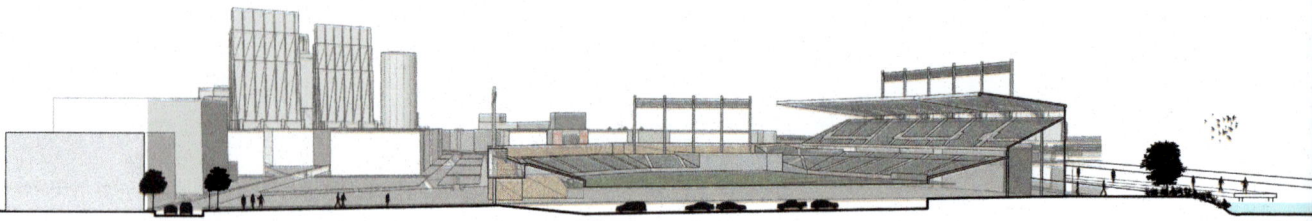

1

Landscape urbanism strategies that fuse ecology and infrastructure can leverage existing models of capital funding. To build urban connectivity through this alliance, while developing new economic models for public spaces, requires *BIG* thinking. Not only is capital management in the form of urban ecology and infrastructure allocation critical, but also the management of programmatic territories requires thinking beyond the framework of designing urbanism through the lens of the landscape. Though public funding is a hallmark of this *BIG* thinking, private partnerships build another form of financial investment. This market investment enhances the programmatic infrastructure.

The land available for *BIG* projects can be unearthed through a creative rethinking of public infrastructure. Cities such as Tampa that have been victimized in the name of "urban renewal", now have the opportunity to right these wrongs. While these vast highway networks have produced many positive results at the interstate transit scale, it has been less successful at the local scale. Paradoxically, these freeways in many ways impede vehicular traffic by disrupting the urban street grid, restricting local movement patterns, and ultimately sullying development opportunities. Not only have these systems of on and off ramps created a disconnect in local traffic patterns, but they have also used-up large tracks of land. The loss of revenue due to this missed opportunity for development is significant. In Tampa, the extended on-ramp and off-ramp system, a collection of highway spurs, cripples the physical continuities of the city. Currently, the 1/3-mile southern spur of I-275 at Exit 44 bypasses potential development land, while disconnecting residential neighborhoods from the Central Business District. The demolition of this spur will liberate 23 acres of land for redevelopment and reinvestment.

Post-demolition, this urban design proposal spurs the development of a neighborhood identity, by the creation of a *BIG* destination in a part of Tampa that, in the past, has operated as purely functional infrastructure. Because Tampa is centrally located between the major populations in St. Petersburg and surrounding communities to the north and east, it sits at the crossroads of many regional economic, civic and cultural opportunities.

1. Stadium for Tampa The Land Available for BIG Projects can be Unearthed Through a Creative Re-thinking of Public Infrastructure.

With 23 acres of new land (post spur demolition), a 21st century baseball stadium for the Tampa Bay Rays, moving the team from St. Petersburg to the north end of the Cultural District in downtown Tampa, provides a new destination and identity. The stadium is nestled within 14 acres of ecological restoration, including wetlands and 1.65 miles of restorative riparian edge as well as the Ashley Street pedestrian-oriented shade boulevard and the river walk, where glimpses into the stadium are afforded. The north and south edges, located at the base of the stadium, act as bio filters for the Hillsborough River. The outdoor stadium is configured to inter-twine with I-275: grandstand seating cantilevers over the highway, while providing amazing views to downtown Tampa, the I-275 southern spur is repurposed for parking underneath the stadium, while additional parking is tucked under the baseball field, and additional surface parking is located under I-275 to the east. Repurposing 1500 parking spaces, this proposal provides 511,499 of square footage of new leasable program.

With at least 81 home games per season, the stadium can draw over 2,340,000 people (30,000 people a game) to downtown. With additional redevelopment property available, this area of Tampa becomes an economic machine through public/private partnership. The location for the stadium will be integrated with new urban fabric, surrounded by commercial, retail and residential buildings with easy access to the Central Business District and Tampa Heights. These amenities and economic potential ameliorate the isolation at the stadium's current location. A new downtown destination spurs job growth and encourages repopulation, extending residential growth south into downtown and business and retail growth north into Tampa Heights.

The area of this project is identified as 'between neighborhoods'; abandoned even by the city's district map. It is NOT part of the Theater District, nor is it part of the Cultural or Central Business District. To reinforce an identity initiated by the new stadium,

the urban design strategy weaves together a series of connective tissues from the central business district to Tampa Heights. These north/south tissues include the following: 1) a broad, pedestrian-scaled tree-lined boulevard at Ashley Street that transitions into a new 'ecological lawn' north of the I-275 (at the existing campus buildings), 2) a link between Franklin Street and the new marina, 3) an extension of the River Walk, 4) lengthen the light rail and add new stops, making it accessible to 80% of the downtown, and 5) the use of the proposed intermodal station to weave parts of the city together, east and west across the new north/south tissue. The new 'ecological lawn', north of I-275, provides a second educational campus to complement the University of Tampa campus. This lawn provides a new front to the river for the group of educational and business programs, while also acting as a bio-filtration transition zone to the Hillsborough River. The lawn extends from the Stetson Law School, and connects into Tampa Heights at the Brewster Technical Center.

The river, though an important amenity to the city, is underutilized, and lacks an influence on city develop-ment. In the Waterworks District, the river is pushed into the land to create a marina. The marina, with twenty, 70' long 2 sided docks, creates prominent water taxi stations visible at the end of the Franklin pedestrian road. The confluence of the extended river walk, the Ashley Street pedestrian boulevard, the Franklin pedestrian road, and the retention and expansion of a wetland north of I-275 come together at this marina. As part of the marina development, a total of 1.65 miles of marshes (8713 linear feet of riparian edge) are provided with a continuous river walk for viewing, walking, running and biking.

Thinking *BIG* requires the introduction of creative urban design strategies. The strategic demolition of highway infrastructure provides opportunities for the redevelopment of critical land along the Hillsbor-ough River, and between disconnected neighbor-hoods. The stadium anchors a variety of new pro-gram elements in a location that is economically viable, as well as ecologically vital. This nexus of

1. Flexibility of Territorial Programs Includes
Multi-modes of Transportation + Multiple Micro-Urban Programs.
2. Baseball Stadium with Program Infrastructure that Offers a Multitude
of Events Within one Building, Occupies Waterfront.

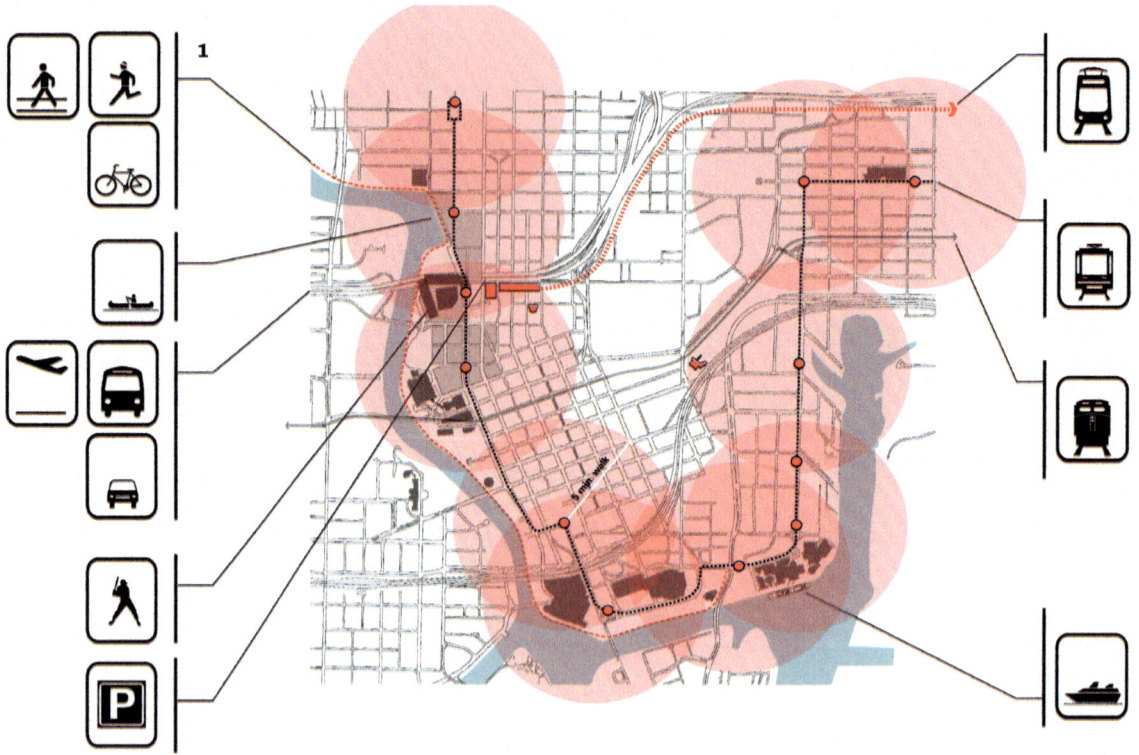

infrastructure and ecology builds neighborhood identity and urban connectivity through a public private partnership.

A strength of the landscape urbanism project type is the flexibility of territorial program. Though somewhat controversial, baseball stadiums create program infrastructure that offer a multitude of events within one building type, including Animal Show, Beer and Wine Tasting, Auto Show, Bingo, Beerfest, Blood Drive, Annual Chili Cookoff, Book fair, Carnival, Cinco De Mayo Salsa Dancing, Celtic Festival, Cheerleading Competition, College Fair, Cultural Exposition, and Collegiate Baseball, to name just a few (from A-C). Considering the length of a typical MLB season, it is conceivable that other programs can occupy the building during 3/4 of the year, with the potential to attract over 150,000 unique non-baseball visitors annually. The economic impact, of which is important to the public funding model.

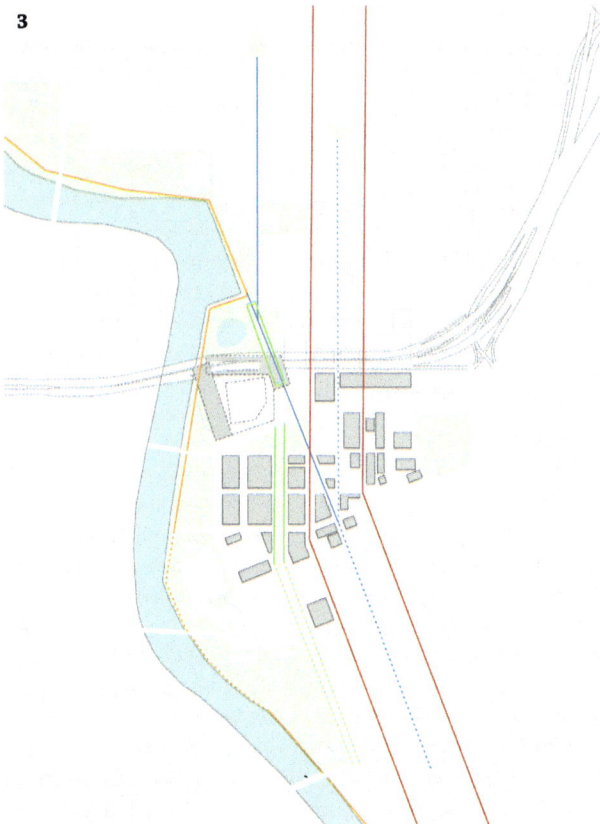

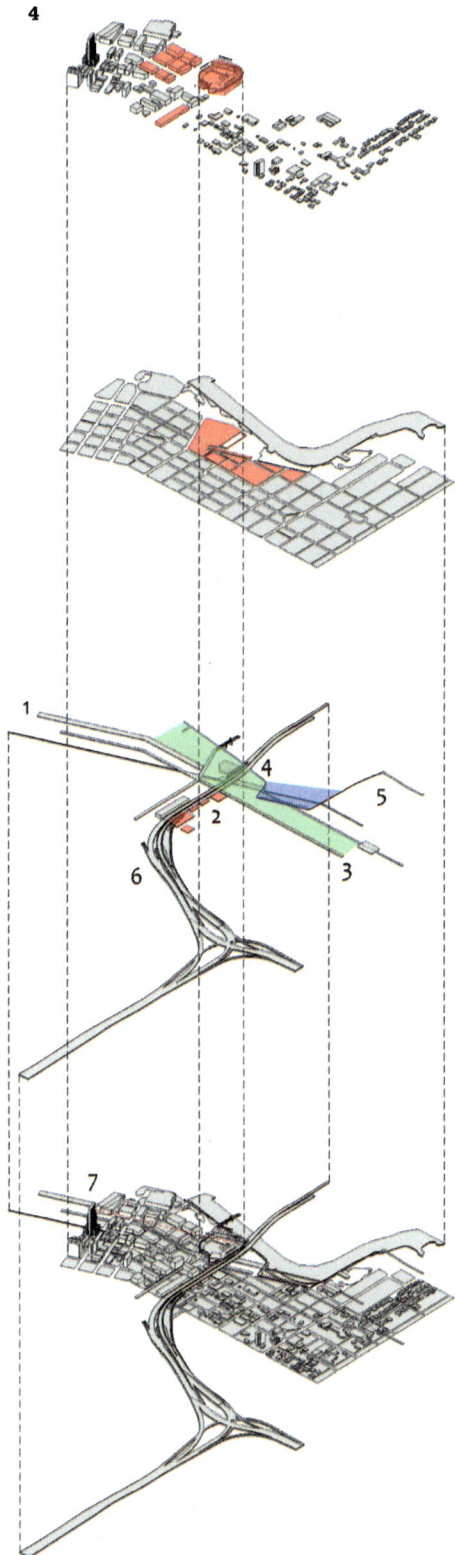

3, 4. Downtown Tampa showing the Spur with the Stadium showing its possible different programmatic functions.

The Spine

Reintegrating Downtown Tampa
with the Waterfront

**Jennifer Williamson
(University of Guelph)**

Guelph, Ontario, Canada

0 50 100   200   500

CONTEXT

The city of Tampa, Florida, has come to the realization that many cities have arrived to as of late - that the city and the landscape are synonymous. Having developed largely as a car-centric and industry oriented city, Tampa is now looking to move away from its current form, and the focus on revitalizing the infrastructure, connectivity and ecology of the downtown core. The Hillsborough River, which traverses the western side of the downtown area, is now the focus of revitalization efforts, which strive to reverse the negative effects that decades of use as an industrial corridor have had on the ecosystem of the river. The gridiron layout of the city responds primarily to the needs of drivers, and collides with the Hillsborough River in a series of dead-end roads and noisy over-passes. The result is a city that is disconnected from the water system that helped to define it, and which has become more successful at transporting run-off pollutants than people to the water's edge.

1. Landscape Ecology is Used as the Catalyst for Improved Pedestrian Circulation, Business Revival, Place-Making and Increased Understanding of Natural Systems.
2-3. Tiers of Native Vegetation Used to Treat the Elevational Change Between Street and Water Level.

1

2

The solution is a new way of looking at the city, not as an island, but as a dynamic and responsive system within the landscape.

Downtown Tampa functions as an inward focused business hub, which sees an influx of people travelling to and from work each day. A recent economic downturn resulted in the closure of businesses throughout the city and along the riverfront. The city is now pockmarked with vacant and foreclosed lots, signs of wear that impact the adjacent businesses and overall moral. The downtown area is composed largely of impermeable surfaces, with a staggering 50% of the core comprised of paved surface parking. The Hillsborough River's vibrant ecosystem, which used to support mussels, oysters and manatees, has been degraded by the implementation of concrete sea walls, pollution from agricultural runoff up stream, and a downtown storm water system which empties directly into the river. This river is part of a large watershed, which feeds into the Tampa Bay, and is prone to sea level fluctuation and flooding. The current River Walk, which runs along the edge of the river, is incomplete and bisected by busy streets and bridges. The challenges of remediating the ecology of the river serve as the platform for the design of a cohesive and functional city.

CONCEPT

The Spine is a reconceptualised vision of the city, which resets the Hillsborough River as the backbone of the city, along which business, transportation, activity and ecology can be organized. The design seeks to use landscape ecology as the catalyst for improved pedestrian circulation, business revival, place making, and an increased public understanding of natural systems. Pedestrian-oriented design and progressive treatment of urban water systems, is central to the proposal, which sees the removal of the degraded sea wall and the thinning of major road arteries, to expand the pedestrian realm. The design is structured around a matrix of ecology and circulation that connects existing and proposed sites along the river and the city's edge.

3

SYMBIOTIC OPPORTUNITIES

The River Walk is the name given to the overarching geometric system, which replaces the existing channelized portion of the Hillsborough River. Juxtaposing wild, untamed natural systems against a rigid, architectural aesthetic, the River Walk weaves a new path system together with re-established native riparian zones. Tiers of native vegetation are held in place with permeable retaining walls, and used to accommodate the vertical grade change between the street level and the water level. Rather than being piped directly into the river, storm water from the streets enters the retention tiers at the top, and infiltrates into each of the subsequent levels before entering the river. During this journey, sediment settles out, and the use of native, phytoremediating species, aid in the filtering of the runoff. The quantity of the water reaching the river will be reduced, and the quality greatly improved. To establish vegetation quickly, floating wetlands fashioned to match the angular style of the tiers are used. Floating wetlands are essentially a growing medium supported by a floating membrane, tethered to the riverbed. The species, emergent and aquatic, will be selected for their water filtering, phytoremediating values, ensuring that the river as well as the runoff is being cleaned. These layers of vegetation retain the function of the sea walls, acting as a buffer to storm surges and sea level rise. Furthermore, the use of softscaping, with its potential for infiltration, and the increased area offered by the

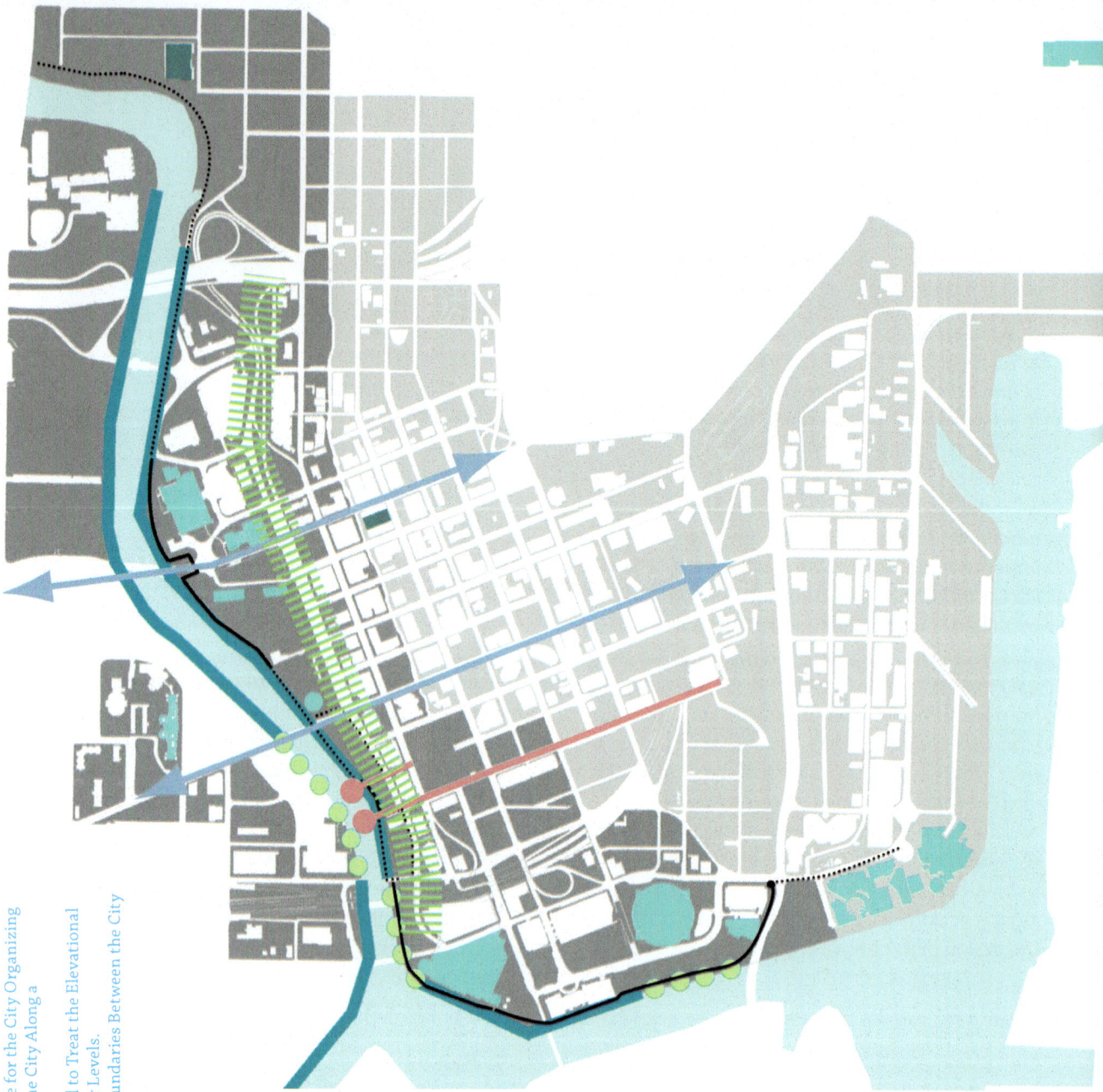

4. The River Serves as a New Spine for the City Organizing the Programmatic Functions of the City Along a Superimposed, Ecological Spine.
5. Tiers of Native Vegetation Used to Treat the Elevational Change Between Street and Water Levels.
6. Dissolving and Blurring the Boundaries Between the City and Nature

4

5

6

set-back tiers, the result is a river edge that is more capable of mitigating the fluctuations in water level. The angular swatches of vegetation provide a diversity of habitats, creating an undulating edge, with areas of sheltered and open water.

SYSTEMS CONNECTED

The path system of the River Walk weaves along the river, branching out and coming together in a sinuous manner, which responds to the points of interest along the route. The path meets the street level at frequent intervals, and serves as a through system for daily commuters, as well as a recreational trail for leisurely activity. It is intended that the points where the River Walk meets the street become revitalized commercial and cultural nodes. The trail also connects several existing cultural sites and open spaces. The Tampa Museum of Art, Curtis Hixon Park and MacDill Park are all situated along the water's edge. The River Walk integrates these isolated features, facilitating place making by bringing the sites together as a unified district or destination. The path system is also interspersed with areas for the docking of water taxis and pleasure crafts, strengthening the identity of the river as an area for activity, and as part of the infrastructure of the city. The introduction of the plant life improves the viability of water sports, including competitive and pleasure rowing, kayaking and canoeing along the river.

BREAKING BOUNDARIES, PROGRESSIVE COLLABORATION

The River Walk seeks to break down the physical boundaries between the city core and the river, the aesthetic contrast between architecture and nature, and the disconnect between people and ecology. Shards of vegetation protrude out into the river and into the city, as a representative fracturing of both. The Tampa Riverwalk is intended to bring nature back into the city, as well as bringing people into close quarters with ecological functions and the landscape. To enhance movement through the city core, major streets with a connection to the river were redesigned as part of a way-finding strategy. Cass Street and Kennedy Boulevard are primary arteries of the city, and have direct lines to the river. To strengthen the connection between the downtown core and the river, these roads undergo a revolution. The road widths are reduced, a traffic calming measure, and the pedestrian walkways widened. New street plantings develop the pedestrian realm, and double as bio-swales for managing storm water runoff and reducing the urban heat island. Green pavement striping and glass aggregate asphalt on the roadwork work in tandem to direct users to the water - to get to the water, follow the green stripes. The playful and vibrant way-finding system injects nature into the core, and solidifies the city's connection to the river.

ADAPTIVE RE-USE, HEIGHTENED PROGRAMMING AND DESTINATION DEVELOPMENT

Building on the theme of breaking-down boundaries and reclaiming the built environment are the Piers. The dead-ends of Washington Street and Whiting Street are extended into the Hillsborough River to function as lookouts and areas with un-programmed activity. The streets transition from asphalt into strips of grasses, which eventually widen to include larger plant material and trees. This transition represents the reclaiming of the city by nature, and the conversion of vehicle spaces into human spaces, and subsequently into natural spaces. The portions of the road, which experience the revitalization, are only at the ends of the streets, which share no connections to adjacent businesses. As such, this new green space is achieved without impacting existing travel routes. Additionally, the Piers are connected with the River Walk, serving as destinations along the route. To avoid the sterilizing effects that smooth, sheer walls can have in an aquatic habitat, rip rap and oyster shell baskets are used to soften the edges, and provide a growing medium for aquatic organisms. Within the context of The Spine, the Piers offer yet another opportunity for restoring the ecosystem of the river, synchronized with revitalizing the human realm.

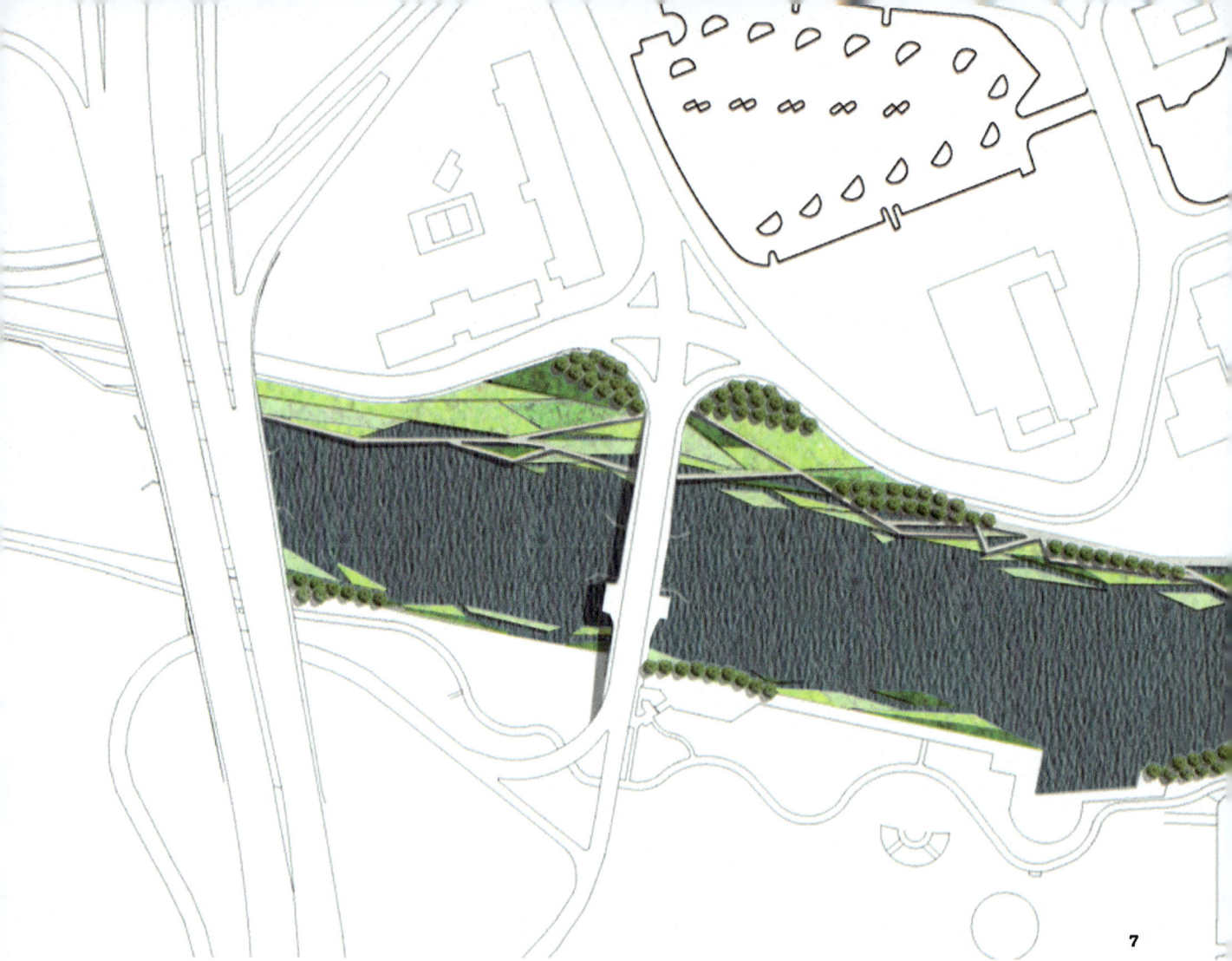

7

8

ECOLOGY INTERPRETED, RELATIONSHIPS ENHANCED

The final component of *The Spine* is the Plaza. Situated on the now vacant lot at the intersection of Ashley Street and Brorein Street, the Plaza is a new public open space, which unites ecology and the public realm. The plaza takes its form from the design of city, playing on the gridiron layout of streets and latticework of buildings. The form of the plaza transitions, much like the Piers, from a strict grid pattern of trees and bioswales, into the angular form shared by the Riverwalk. This, again, is a nod to the efforts of breaking down the boundaries between the city and the river, and improving the physical and psychological connections between the people and the waterfront. Again, ecology is a vehicle of design and infrastructure, as this site functions as a storm water filtering system. At the top of the site, running parallel to Ashley Street, is a cascading fountain, which spills over the sides and falls into a series of tiered retention gardens. It is intended that the water feeding the fountain be drawn from the Hillsborough River, and that storm water from the city be piped into the retention gardens as opposed to directly into the river. These retention gardens act as bioswales, removing sediment and pollution, by allowing larger particles to settle out, while finer contaminants are filtered by the wetland vegetation of the gardens. The water drops from one level to the next before finally being released back into the river, in its improved state. Elevated above these bio filtration gardens, are strips of paving with a network of trees. These trees are housed in concealed tree wells to give the illusion of growing out of the wetland or out of the paving, and help to control the soil moisture.

FLEXIBLE SPACE, VERSATILE USE

Seating areas located beneath the canopy offer visitors places to rest, contemplate and meet, while enjoying the gurgle of water and the proximity to active ecological processes. The site slopes down towards the river and connects with the River Walk. Moveable seating and tables are provided for gathering and passive recreation, and an associated un-programmed open space provides the potential site for food vendors and outdoor performances. This site is intended both as a resting point along the River Walk, and as an individual destination, a place to spend lunch breaks, or a quiet evening. Access to green spaces such as these are considered to be rejuvenating for users of the space, and help to improve quality of life and can contribute to happier and more productive lifestyles. While the primary focus of *The Spine* has been on remediating the ecosystem of the Hillsborough River, the resulting environment also positively impacts the quality of life of city dwellers and their guests.

CONCLUSION

Tampa, Florida, is part of the landscape. The existing car-privileged and inward focused layout and channelized Hillsborough River have resulted in a degraded ecosystem, a lack of connectivity with the water, and an archaic infrastructure. *The Spine* uses progressive landscape ecology as a way to re-establish the city as a functioning component within the surrounding natural system. The River Walk is the uniting feature of the design concept, focusing on replacing the dilapidated sea walls with native plantings and remediated aquatic habitat. Skirting through this new riparian zone is a path system, which transports pedestrians and cyclists along the river's edge, in close confines with nature, and connects with existing and future sites of interest. With the implementation of inventive way-finding systems throughout the city, the accessibility and presence of the river is improved throughout. The Piers and the Plaza build on the theme of incorporating infrastructure and ecology within public open spaces, and breaking down the barriers between the city and its inhabitants, and the river. In improving the sense of place and unity, the design redefines the river's edge as a unified district. This vein of culture and green space has the potential to stimulate new economic activity, improve public wellness and livability of the city. No longer an island within a landscape, *the Spine* offers the City of Tampa a holistic solution, which brings its inhabitants back into contact with a restored and vibrant ecosystem and establishes a new focus for the city, the Hillsborough River.

Reclaim Tampa

Lisa Verbon (MScStudent Landscape Architecture and Planning, Wageningen University), Dual porosity filtration: Marina Bergen Jensen (Copenhagen University)

Wageningen, Netherlands

Scenario Economic Growth

BASIS	Topography, flood zones and increase in building developments
CAPACITY	2-hour 25-year rain event (120mm)
GOAL	A green framework which enables dense, high-quality build developments in the higher parts of the landscape.

PERMEABLE CITY GRID: RETENTION LAKES
Water storage and purification
Stimulate building developments in higher parts of the landscape

PERMEABLE CITY GRID: GREEN STREETS AND POCKET PARK
Water storage and purification
Pedestrian friendly environment

FRESHWATER WETLAND
Water storage and purification
Natural park space

TIDAL STRIP
Water purification and flood protection
Natural park space

American Coastal Cities are Unprepared for Hurricanes

Recent hurricane events Katrina (2005) and Sandy (2012) demonstrate that North American cities are unable to deal with heavy rainfall and storm surges. Until now, these city developments always have been steered by economic and technical development. This created a footloose process of urbanization, which neglects the natural circumstances within the environment. (McHarg, 1969) If we keep building this way, more flood disasters will be inevitable. If a 100-year flood were to strike Tampa Bay today, this would damage 14% of the building stock, resulting in a structural damage cost of $10,893 million. (Tampa Bay Regional Planning Council and Hillsborough County, 2008).

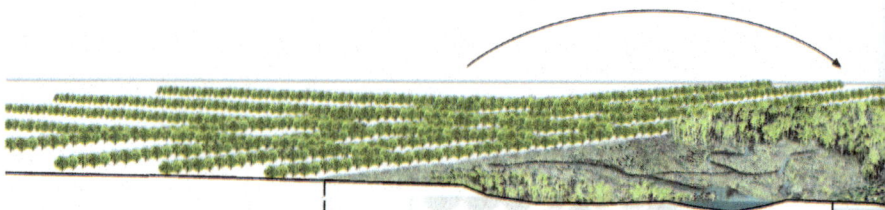

PERMEABLE CITY GRID

infiltration & purification I

100-year floodline

FRESHWATER WETLAND

retention & purification II

springtide

Nature and size of the stormwater transport structure corresponds to the street. It acts as a shade structure for cyclists and pedestrians and can be linked to public infrastructure.

In case of large sized blocks, a secondary network is integrated in the blocks. The city is made more pedestrian friendly by creating shortcuts for pedestrians only.

Combine multiple blocks to create large water bodies or infiltration areas. Water can be stored and used for irrigation in the dry season. These attractive areas can be used to steer urban developments.

Multifuntional blocks combine water storage with parking, play or food production. Water is purified and cascaded between the different functions, eg. hydroponic farming or water play. Vegetation enhances the microclimate.

Parts of blocks are transformed into water storage and infiltration areas. This creates more intimate spaces like shaded seating or play areas. Infiltration boxes are used to increase storage and infiltration capacity when there is a limited amount of space.

To increase biodiversity, use a variety of native species in multiple layers on top of each other (groundcover, shrubs, trees). Choose especially species which provide nectar, berries and nuts to wildlife. Also introduce rare species.

To control erosion, chose plants with an extensive root system to stabilize soil, especially in swales. Prevent bare soil by using groundcover such as graminoids, wildflowers, vines and ferns.

Right plant at right place: select for right soil (bog, clay, sand) and hydological condition (wet, regularly flooded, dry). For raingardens and swales, use plants with a large amplitude in order to tolerant longer periods of drought and short periods of flooding.

Prevent salt water entering the wetland during a storm, because still standing salt water kills the trees. Therefore, create a levee between the tidal strip and the wetland. Hammock vegetation will naturally occur on this levee.

Cascade the water in bays. The first bay captures most of the suspended solids from the urban run-off. The next bays acts as overflow basins in case of heavy rainfall.

Create curved streams instead of straight ones to increase the distance and therefore time for water to travel which leads to optimal removal of nutrients.

Improve predator access for fish and water insects to limit mosquitoes: create open water and an open structure of diverse vegetation for a consistent water flow.

Use sustainable harvest to create diverse stages of succession within the wetland which enhances biodiversity.

Show that some one is caring for this green area by providing order in the natural chaos, for example by creating sharp edges or by adding signs, benches and pathways.

Enable access to the wetland. The type of path, especially its width and materials, influence the tactile experience. Pathways can also have a more adventurous character by introducing elements from climbing forests.

TIME TO TAKE ACTION

To change current practices, is to change how people think. With a visionary design, this project aims to show a different way of city development. Hopefully, this will inspire people to develop holistic, long-term plans for our future cities.

This project takes the landscape as a starting point for the design of the city, which has two main consequences. First, urban developments should be designed to correspond to the abiotic and biotic circumstances in the landscape. For example, skyscrapers should be built on sandy soils and not in peat areas. Secondly, the design of the city cannot be a static master plan. As a landscape, it is continuously shaped by natural processes, such as sea level rise. It should therefore consist of a strategy based on a model with guidelines (or design principles). In this way, you can deal with (unexpected) change, coming from nature, as well as our society.

TIDAL STRIP

storm surge protection & purification III

For salt marsh vegetation to establish, create planes of 0.0 to 1.0 meter above mean sea level (MSL). For mangrove trees to establish, create planes of 0.3 to 0.6 meter above MSL.

Create banks ranging from 0.5 to 2.5 meter below MSL for seagrasses to establish on. Vegetation protects against erosion, protects mainland shorelines from tidal energy, storm surge, and wave forces, filters pollutants, and absorbs atmospheric CO2.

Place hard surface material and a source of calciumcarbonate (e.g. limestone) in the river for to create oyster reefs. The reefs have to be parallel to the shoreline to dissipate wave energy. They also decrease coastal erosion and increase habitat for fish species.

Create creeks in the salt marsh and mangrove planes to enable the nutrient-rich water from the river to enter and fertilize the tidal strip. Marine life also depends on these flows.

Exaggerate the topography to reduce wave energy during a storm. The bankfaces consist of sea oats (Uniola paniculata). This grass is deeply rooted and protects the banks against erosion.

Enable access for kayaks and pedestrians in parts of the mangrove and salt marsh in order for people to experience the nature from up close. A narrow pedestrian path intensifies your experience of nature.

Create landmarks and views towards the river and the city to enable orientation and create a feeling of spaciousness.

THE NUSS MODEL: HOLISTIC DEVELOPMENT FOR AMERICAN COASTAL CITIES

The NUSS (Nature and Urban Storm Water Synergy) model integrates city development with abiotic and biotic processes in the landscape.

To regulate large and polluted quantities of water inside the landscape, the NUSS model integrates two theories, namely the infiltration model of Tjallingii (2012) and the storm water treatment train approach. Each theory addresses a different important aspect of storm water management. The infiltration model of Tjallingii (2012) provides general guidelines about how to deal with the amount water inside the city, based on the soil type. The storm water treatment train provides guidelines about how you can improve the water quality by cascading it in a 'train' of purification solutions.

THE 3 PARTS OF THE NUSS MODEL

The NUSS model consists of 3 parts: the permeable city grid, the freshwater wetland and the tidal strip. The division of these areas is based on the topography and soil type of the landscape. The permeable city grid can be laid out on the higher, sandier parts of the land-scape. Here the water is stored, purified and infiltrated into the ground. By doing this, an important drink water resource, the Florida Aquifer, is recharged. The freshwater wetland is located on the lower-lying sandy, clayey or peaty parts. The wetland is capable of absorbing large quantities of water during an extreme rain event. Furthermore, it is very capable of increasing the quality of this water due to the amount of microbial activity. The last part, the tidal strip, is situated in the lowest areas, which inundate during springtide. Here run-off mixes with water from the river and the sea. This creates a dynamic habitat where the levels of salt, nutrient and water change all the time. The vegetation and animals inside this habitat buffer these changes and purify the water at the same time.

ECONOMIC SCENARIOS DETERMINE FUNCTIONS

Each part of the NUSS model will provide unique opportunities for city-related functions. However, many different developments can occur, resulting in an infinite number of possible future outcomes. Therefore, I only show the most extreme outcomes by using scenarios. These scenarios will be based on the econo-my as the financial market steers urban developments in the USA. As a result there will be two scenarios, one based on economic growth and one based on econom-ic decline. Policy makers and city officials can use these scenarios to promote certain developments, depending on the economic climate.

Nature and water have different roles in each scenario. When the economy is growing, buildings pop-up quickly. The green-blue structure will facilitate this growth. When the economy declines, vacant areas arise

inside the city. These areas can be used for food and biomass production in lean times. Both scenarios show that nature is indispensable in the functioning of an urban system as it cleans and buffers storm water run-off and provides many other benefits.

PART 1: PERMEABLE CITY GRID

In the scenario economic growth, the transformation starts by the development of retention lakes. These lakes store and purify large amounts of water. At the same time, they act as a buffer, providing water for irrigation in times of drought. These large, attractive lakes can be used to steer urban development. They lure businesses to the safe, high parts of the landscape, and away from the dangerous floodplains of the river. The city government can co-fund these lakes together with private investors which can built offices and high-density housing along the waterside. The lakes will provide an attractive area for people as well as wildlife.

Connected to the lakes, is a network of green streets. The swales inside the streets will transport, store and infiltrate rainwater. Smaller infiltration elements like rain gardens and ponds are connected to the swale network. The vegetation will mitigate the urban heat island effect, and create a pedestrian and bicycle network. The green streets and parks go hand-in-hand with high-density building developments and public transport. In this way, a high-quality living and working environment is created, which promotes a healthy lifestyle. In the economic decline scenario, the green framework of the permeable city grid will facilitate local food and energy production. The swale network captures water and transports it to natural basins, where it is purified. Various agricultural grassroots developments will use this water. For example, in moveable fish tanks and hydroponic installations. The water is circulated for optimal use of the nutrients. Furthermore, this process of cycling the water ensures that water is available during periods of drought. The water is also used for irrigating the crops.

PART 2: FRESHWATER WETLAND

In the economic growth scenario, the city officials should focus on developing the low-lying areas into wetlands. The freshwater wetland can be constructed as a city park. The topography is exaggerated, creating a diverse area with open water and levees. Groups of trees are composed to create views over the water. Boardwalks guide you through this composed landscape, where you can encounter various fish, reptiles and birds. Buildings are sparse and build on poles or floaters in order to deal with changing water levels. The wetland vegetation creates an idyllic background for enterprises like restaurants.

In the economic decline scenario, the freshwater wetland functions as a production area for food and biomass. Nutrients from the storm water run-off are taken up by cypress trees and reed. Through a process of decay and denitrification, these nutrients are taken up by fish. Sustainable harvests of the timber, reed and fish prevents the wetland from becoming too eutrophic. The wetland can be managed by establishing a collective, so that tools, labor and knowledge can be easily shared.

The transition from the wetland to the tidal strip consists of a belt of hammocks. These higher grounds protect the freshwater wetland from storm surges. In times of economic growth, these higher grounds offer a unique setting for recreational facilities. In times of economic decline, these higher areas will offer intimate, quiet spaces with a wide view over the wetland or tidal strip.

PART 3: TIDAL STRIP

By crossing the hammock belt, you enter the tidal strip. Here, you can find dense mangrove forests and wide fields of salt marsh grasses. When the groundwork is done and the substrate is put in place, these pioneer species establish themselves spontaneously. The result is an impressive piece of Florida's nature, which you can explore in a kayak or small boat.

In times of economic growth, boardwalks can be created which provide safe and dry pathways in this dynamic wet area. Explorative people will discover springs and possibly encounter a manatee. These friendly creatures are drawn to the mineral-rich spring water. By looking up, you can spot one of the many birds, which use this area for resting and feeding during their annual migration. Another way to enter the mangrove is from the water. Small yachts have the possibility to dock along the river. Here, somewhat hidden behind the bush, you will find a floating restaurant, where you can dine while admiring the reflections of the sun over the river. This restaurant is one of the many amenities which are located along the river; the heart of the tidal strip.

In the economic decline scenario, the tidal strip will

function as a food source. Many fish, shellfish and crabs thrive here, which can be caught on a small scale to be sold on local markets. Not much will be built during the period of aneconomic decline, so only a few paths provide access to this remote natural area. If you have a kayak, you will be able to enter it and come into close contact with the fish, birds and manatees. In this way you will truly experience the wilderness of Florida.

DESIGN PRINCIPLES TO TRANSLATE THE NUSS STRATEGY INTO A DESIGN

In order to translate the NUSS strategy into concrete design, design principles are developed. These principles will inform city planners and urban designers about how they will get the most out of each intervention. Solutions developed with the NUSS model will not only improve water quality and prevent floods, they will also improve biodiversity, provide recreational activities and enhance spatial experience.

INCORPORATING NATURAL PROCESSES

The scenarios incorporate sea level rise, by using the dynamic 100-year flood line as starting point. The first part of the NUSS model, the permeable city grid, is located above this flood line. The other two parts are located below the flood line, e.g. the wetlands. As the 100-year flood line moves inland in the future, the wetlands will also move inland.

CALCULATING STORAGE CAPACITIES

The storm water system in both scenarios is designed to deal with a large storm, which occurs on average every 25 years (a 2hour 25year rain event). So, every year there is a chance of 1/25, thus 4%, that this rain event occurs. Therefore, the chance on a larger rain event, which will cause local floods, is less than 4%.

In order to deal with the 25-year rain event, all the interventions need to be realized. It is possible that there are situations in which this level of implementation cannot be reached. As a minimum, urban storm water interventions should be able to deal with a 5-year rain event. (Jensen et al., 2010) In this situation, the risk of local floods is 1/5, thus 20%. To deal with the run-off of the 5-year rain event, 78% of the interventions need to be realized. In this way, there is some flexibility in the plan if one chooses to develop some areas otherwise.

Another option is to shift between the development of the wetlands or permeable city grid. When more space inside the city is transformed into swales and rain gardens, less space is need for the wetlands and vice versa. In this way, you do not increase the risk on local floods.

BENEFITS OF WORKING WITH NATURE INSIDE THE CITY

In the USA, waterfront development occurring in the form of linear parks and boulevards is very popular. The danger of this phenomenon is that each city becomes alike. The NUSS model can enhance the city's identity by introducing a landscape identity. Site-specific landscape elements, such as natural springs, native vegetation and local materials are central in the design. In Tampa, 70% of the city trees are represented by 8 species. (Andreu et al., 2008) The NUSS model introduces more than 60 native tree species, bringing the atmosphere of the surrounding natural areas into the city. When walking under the elegant palm trees or giant oaks covered with moss, you feel that you are in Florida!

Another danger of the waterfront development scenario, is that the public space will only support formal activities related to water and nature. On the Riverwalk, you can walk along the water, but cannot touch it. Inside the city, children play in concrete water features dominated by the smell of chlorine. When I applied the NUSS model to Tampa, I found out that there is a large potential for generating everyday experiences that bring us in close contact with water and nature. Both scenarios create tactile, informal experiences, each in their own way.

Current waterfront developments do not deal with the worldwide loss of wetland habitat. Both scenarios show a large potential for increasing biodiversity on a regional scale by creating new natural habitats inside the city. A large part of these habitats consist of freshwater and tidal wetlands, one of the most diverse ecosystems on our planet. In Downtown Tampa, 180 hectares of freshwater

wetland and 70 hectares of tidal wetland is created. If the NUSS model would be implemented in the whole city of Tampa, the wetlands would be doubled in size. Furthermore, there is a large potential for developing wetlands as integrative part of the city in the southwest of Tampa. Further research is needed about the integration of these wetlands inside neighborhoods.

START TODAY AND LEARN ALONG THE WAY

The NUSS model can be used as basis for a step-by-step strategy, which transforms your city into a hurricane-proof, environmental-friendly, and attractive city. The transformation can be seen as organic growth. It starts with a pilot project in an area, which has potential to show of the benefits for recreation, sustainable transport, food production or real estate development. Once this pilot project is developed, it will function as a main artery, where other projects can be to linked to. Transforming the city in phases has several advantages. First, you can learn from each step, applying the knowledge in the next phase. Therefore, failures, especially in the early phases, can be seen as unique learning opportunities. Secondly, the construction can start today instead of tomorrow. Starting with a small project requires less money and only a small group of

enthusiastic people. Once the changes become visible, people will become inspired to invest in similar projects.

APPLYING THE NUSS MODEL TO OTHER CITIES

The NUSS model and its design principles can be applied to Tampa, but also to American coastal cities with similar problems, see table below. By reflecting on the scenarios of Tampa, I want to point out the two most important conditions, which are needed for the NUSS model to succeed.

First, the NUSS model can only be applied to a city with a certain topography. A considerate amount of relatively low-lying space (eg floodplains) is needed in order to create the wetlands. Depending on the resources available, the topography can be altered, creating a patchwork of higher and lower lying areas. At a minimum, some levees (the hammock belt) should be created to protect the low-lying freshwater wetland from storm surges.

Secondly, the NUSS model can be best applied to a city, which is (partly) built on soils with a relatively high infiltration rate, because it influences the size of the interventions of the permeable city grid. If

NUSS model can be applied to:		
Tampa	Seattle	Boston
Jacksonville	Portland	New York
Fort Lauderdale	San Francisco	Philadelphia
Miami	Los Angeles	Washington

the infiltration rate is lower than K=10-4 m/s, the interventions need a large amount of space in order to store the water until it infiltrates. This can be a problem in cities where space is scarce. Therefore, the NUSS model is best applied to cities lie (partly) on sandy or loamy soils. Cities which lie fully on peaty and clayey soils will need to use another model.

Sources:

Andreu, Michael G., Melissa H. Friedman, Shawn M. Landry and Robert J. Northrop. 2008. City of Tampa Urban Ecological Analysis 2006-2007. Final Report to the City of Tampa, April 24, 2008. City of Tampa, Florida.

Jensen, M.B. A. Backhaus and O. Fryd, 2010. Storm water management in the urban landscape – overview of elements and their dimensioning. Forest and Landscape, Faculty of Life Sciences, University of Copenhgen.

McHarg, I.L. 1969. Design with nature. Garden City, N.Y., Published for the American Museum of Natural History [by] the Natural History Press.

Tampa Bay Regional Planning Council (TBRPC), 2008. Hurricane Guide: Official Guide for the Tampa Bay Area. http://www.usfpd.usf.edu/hurricane_guide.pdf

Tjallingii, SP. 2012: Water flows and urban planning. Ch. 4 in: Bueren, E. van, H.van Bohemen, L. Itard & H. Visscher (eds.) Sustainable Urban Environments – An Ecosystems Approach. Springer.

Jurors

Charles Waldheim
Principal, Urban Agency; John E. Irving Professor and Former Chair of the Department of Landscape Architecture at the Harvard University Graduate School of Design

Chris Reed
Principal of Stoss Landscape Urbanism; Associate Professor in Practice of Landscape Architecture at the Harvard University Graduate School of Design

Margaret Crawford
Professor of Architecture, Urban Design and Planning in the College of Environmental Design at the University of California, Berkeley

Juhani Pallasmaa
Arkkitehtitoimisto Juhani Pallasmaa; Former Professor of architecture and Dean at the Helsinki University of Technology. Ruth & Norman Moore Visiting Professor at Washington University, Plym Distinguished Professor at the University of Illinois at Urbana-Champaign

Chad Oppenheim
Principal of Oppenheim Architecture + Design, Miami, Florida, Adjunct professor of Architecture at Florida International University

Lisa J. Montelione
City of Tampa Councilwoman Montelione represents District 7, which encompasses New and North Tampa. The area includes some of Tampa's most prominent assets.

Laurie Potier-Brown
Laurie Potier-Brown is both a registered Landscape Architect and a certified Planner. She is a Landscape Architect at the City of Tampa

Ray Chiaramonte
Mr. Chiaramonte is the Former Executive Director of the Hillsborough County Planning Commission and Metropolitan Planning Organization - the long-range transportation planning agency for Hillsborough County and currently the Executive Director of TBARTA (Tampa Bay Area Regional Transportation Authority)

Emily Meeker O'Mahoney
Mrs. O'Mahoney is the Former President of the Florida Chapter of the American Society of Landscape Architects. Partner at Gentile Glas Holloway O'Mahoney & Associates (2GHO)

Editor/Author

Shannon Bassett Shannon Bassett is an architect and urban designer. Her research, teaching, writing and practice operate at the intersection of architecture, urban design and ecological systems. She teaches both undergraduate, as well as graduate design studios in both architecture, as well as urban design. She also teaches a graduate research seminar entitled, Landscape and Ecology as Urbanism.

Her writing on both China's explosive urbanization and its changing landscape, as well as shrinking cities and the post-industrial landscape in North America, has been published in Topos, Urban Flux (Beijing), Canadian Architect, Garten + Landschaft and Land-scape Architecture China. Her design research has been exhibited both nationally and internationally, including at the Hong Kong and Shenzhen Bi-City Biennale of Urbanism and Architecture (2012) and was featured in the ensuing book publication, "Learning from Tri-ciprocal Cities: The time, the place, the people." She was awarded a National Endowment for the Arts grant for (re)stitch TAMPA, the publication (Re)stitch Tampa Riverfront-Designing the Post-War Coastal American City through Ecologies" ensued from this research platform. Her design practice has included designing an urban design master plan and

study for an urban artist colony on 42-acre site, the Village of the Arts in Bradenton, Florida as well as a series of speculative design studies for the City of Tampa Riverwalk for the City of Tampa.

She has lectured internationally, as well as run design research studios in China collaborating with the Tongji College of Architecture and Urban Planning, the Tianjin School of Architecture and most recently, Turenscape-College of Architecture and Landscape Architecture, Peking University in both Beijing and Anhui province,with a focus on the rural urbanism of Village Planning or "rurbanism". She served as an elected board member of the International Associa-tion for China Planning (IACP) for two consecutive terms 2011-2015. She holds a Masters of Architecture in Urban Design from the Harvard Graduate School of Design and a Bachelors of Architecture with Distinc-tion from Carleton University in Ottawa, Canada. While at Harvard she was a Research and Teaching Assistant for the Center for Urban Development Studies, later the Institute for International Urban Development, assisting with the research for the publication "Financing Urban Shelter : Global Report on Human Settlement" for the United Nations.

Competition Participants

---

*   Competition Winner Schemes

**   Honorable Mention Schemes

*** Additional Selected Proposals

Activating The Voids
Team: Fernando Munilla, Faculty Advisor
Savannah College of Art and Design Team Members:
Chandler Noah, Rajiv Bachan
Location: Savannah, Georgia, USA

Castoridae Morphologies
Team: Studio JEFRE
Team Members: Jeffrey Manuel
Location: Orlando, Florida, USA

Celebrating City Life
Team: Michael Jagodzinski, Wroclaw University of Technology,
Faculty of Architecture
Location: Wroclaw, POLAND

Celebrating Tropical Tampa
Team: Miriam Gusevich, The Catholic University of America
Team Members: Miriam Gusevich, Jay Kabriel, Peter Miles, Paul Schilder,
Location: Washington, DC, USA

**The Center of Tampa: Territory of Systemic
and Ecological Development**
Team: Ural State Academy of Architecture and Arts (USAAA),
Andrew Pechyonkin-Faculty Advisor
Team Members: Andrew Pechyonkin, Valdimir Spiridonov, Leonid Smirnov,
Vladimir Blinov, Veronika Kravchenko, Ksenia Sharova, Polina Urchenko
Location: Ekaterinburg, RUSSIA

City Flux
Team: PH6 design lab
Team Members: Yoonchul Cho
Location: Beijing, CHINA

Ecological Re-Encroachment
Team: 10 Design
Team Members: Ted Givens
Location: Hong Kong

* **Flowscape. Visions for a New Urban Estuary**
Team: Group Han Associates
Team Members: Michael Chaveriat, Yikyu Choe,
Myung Kweon Park
Location: New York City, NY, USA

Green Re-stitching
Team: James Fox
Location: Lakeland, Florida, USA

hydroLogic
Team: HWK
Team Members: Benjamin Waldo, Veronica Keefer
Location: Minneapolis, Minnesota, USA

Live Tampa!
Team: Fernando Munilla-Faculty Advisor,
Savannah College of Art and Design
Team Members: Steven Fedak, Christopher Epps
Location: Savannah, Georgia, USA

** **Pleating Tampa. Pleat, Re-pleat, Repeat**
Team: OH-LA Collaborative
Team Members: Cynthia Anderson, Angela Bushong,
Elizabeth Lagedrost, Susan Noblet,
Location: Columbus + Toledo, Ohio and Los Angeles,
California, USA

**Pulses-Syncopating Urban Interludes
Sustaining Active Networks**
Team: Meghan C. Mick-Faculty Advisor Florida A+M
School of Architecture
Team Members: Robert Bogle, Adrian Carter,
James Eisele, Rachel Marshall, Sonia Ranjbari
Location: Tallahassee, Florida, USA

*** **Reclaim Tampa**
Team: Lisa Verbon (MScStudent Landscape Architecture
and Planning, Wageningen University)
Dual porosity filtration: Marina Bergen Jensen,
Copenhagen University
Location: Wageningen, Netherlands

Reduce Reuse Amuze
Team: Fernando Munilla-Savannah College of Art
and Design
Team Members: Jessie Catnacci, Candice Alinovich
Location: Savannah, Georgia, USA

** **Rehydrate Tampa**
Team: Bryan Hanes, Studio Bryan Hanes
Location: Philadelphia, Pennsylvania, USA

Rerooting Downtown
Team: DA City
Team Members: Aria Ritz Finkelstein
and Deanna Murphy
Location: Atlanta, Georgia, USA

* **(re) Stitch (re) Silience**
Team: Mola + Winkelmueller Architekten GmbH BDA
(Germany)
Team Members: Mola+Winkelmueller Architekten
GmbH BDA-Luis Mola, Astrid Kantzenbach-Mola,
Israel Moreno Torrez, Pilar Gomez Cabellero,
Miguel Cabezas Prudencio

In partnership with: Miguel Prados Sanchez and Pablo
Benitez Adame Arquitectos-Miguel Prados Sanchez,
Pablo Benitez Adame

Local Contact Engineers and Planners:
Genesis Group, Tampa, Florida, Kevin Mineer,
Craig Anderson, Kyle Thornton, Bruce T. Kaschyk,
Jim Gilman, Local environmental and regulatory
research

Environmental Consultants:
Kronawitter Urban Ecology, New York and Berlin
Lukas Kronawitter

Concept Development, Urban ecology, SUDS concept,
climate change adaption:
JFS Engineering, New Jersey
Joe Schaffer

Water management, SUDS calculation, feasibility
and systems analysis:
Buro Happold, Berlin Office
Zareen Sethna, Bill Wilson
SUDS and UHI research

Landscape Consultants:
Kraft-Wehberg Landscape Architecture
and Development
Hans Hermann Kraft

Spcial thanks to:
Marc Russell at the EPA Gulf Ecology Group Division
for local environmental data.
Kevin Mineer at Genesis Group for local planning
information and critical input.
Location: Berlin, Germany

(re)stitch Tampa
Team: Cypres Associate Landscape Architect
Team Members: Soraya Meftah (Landscape Architect),
Jean-Yves Marie (Project Manager), Emma Ayouni
(Urbaniste), Moez Askri (Architect)
Location: Ariana Tunis, Tunisia

(re)stitch Tampa
Team: W+G
Team Members: Wendy Yang, Gustavo Colmenares
Location: New Haven, Connecticut, USA

(re)stitch Tampa Waterfront
Team: LandinDesign
Team Members: Michael T. Smith
Location: West Palm Beach, Florida, USA

Retro-fitting Tampa-Hillsborough River
Team: Planstatt Senner-Planner Group Senner
Team Members: Annette Kastka, Tina Heckler, Johann
Senner, Ole Kuster, Tom Guglielmo
Location: Ueberlingen, Germany and Fort Meyers,
Florida, USA

** **(re)stitch Tampa. The Sub-urban Mix**
Team: arki-lab
Team Members: Jeanette W. Frisk and Rasmus W. Frisk
Location: Copenhagen, Denmark

** **Shifting Currents**
Team: Christopher Fannin-Hok
Team Members: Barry Day
Location: Hong Kong

*** **The Spine. Reintegrating Downtown Tampa
with the Waterfront**
Team: Jennifer Williamson, Faculty Advisor Professor
Sean Kelly, School of Environmental Design and Rural
Development, (Landscape Architecture), University
of Guelph, Canada
Location: Guelph, Ontario, Canada

*** **Spur On / Spur Off. Ecology / Infrastructure /
Connectivity + Economy**
Team: Mo Zell-bauenstudio with Keith Hayes
Location: Milwaukee, Wisconsin, USA

* **Stitches Fabrics**
Team: Chris Webb and Amarja Chhapwale
Webb-archyrsalis
Location: Mumbai, India

*** **Streets. Branches of the River**
Team: TaeKyung Kim, Harvard University
Location: Cambridge, MA, USA

Symbiosis
Team: Design Workshop
Team Members: Vikas Mehta, Shawn Landry,
Thao Nguyen and Alberto Rodriguez
Location: Tampa, Florida, USA

** **Symbiosis - Ri-verizing Tampa**
Team: Vinod Kadu
Location: Port Richey, Florida, USA

Tampa Downtown Towards New Parks
Team: Cao Mengxing, School of Architecture Tsinghua
University
Location: Beijing, China

*** **Tampa (Eco) Grid**
Team: Feriel Mestiri and Xuan Lam Nguyen (Student
at Ecole Nationale Superieure d'architecture Paris val
de Seine)
Location: Paris, France

Tampa (Re)stitch
Team: Landstrom
Team Members: Roger Landstrom
Location: Noosa Heads, Queensland, Australia

Tampa River Gardens
Team: Kaleigh Hastings, University of Florida
Location: Gainseville, Florida, USA

Untitled
Team: Keneshov Tolobai Seydakmatovich, Kyrgyz State
University of Construction
Team Members: Djamankulov Edil Muratbekovich,
Apyshev Ulukbek Kalybekovich, Abdykadyrov Dilshat
Rustamovich
Location: Bishkek City, Kyrgyzstan

**Urban Design Conception of the Strategic
Development of Tampa**
Team: Keneshov Tolobai Seydakmatovich-Kyrgyz State
University of Construction
Team Members: Sasykeev Ulanbek Tolosunovich,
Turgumbekov Aibek Turgumbekovich, Omurkanova
Aizaada Kamchybekovna
Location: Bishkek City, Kyrgyzstan

Urban-Kinesis
Team: Fernando Munilla Faculty Advisor, Savannah
College of Art and Design
Team Members: Ana Hercules, Eric O'Neill
Location: Savannah, Georgia, USA

Published by
Actar Publishers, New York, Barcelona
www.actar.com

Editor and Primary Author
Shannon Bassett

Graphic Design and Digital Production
Papersdoc SL

Copy editing and proofreading
Shannon Bassett

ISBN: 978-19-40291-52-9
Library of Congress Control Number:
2016946867

Distribution
Actar D, Inc.

New York
440 Park Avenue South, 17th Floor
New York, NY 10016, USA
+1 2129662207
salesnewyork@actar-d.com

Barcelona
Roca i Batlle 2
08023 Barcelona, SPAIN
+34 933 282 183
eurosales@actar-d.com

Published on November 2016